THE BIBLICAL PROPHETS:

A Summary of Their Life and Times

Stephen M. Collins

Publisher's Name: Stephen Collins

ISBN: 978-1-962142-98-4

Table of Contents

Chapter 1: *What Is a Prophet?*.. *1*

Chapter 2: *The God and gods of Israel and the Near East* 6

Chapter 3: **Abel**.. **10**

Chapter 4: *Abraham* *12*

Chapter 5: *Moses* *17*

Chapter 6: *Miriam* *22*

Chapter 7: *Aaron* *25*

Chapter 8: *Balaam*... *27*

Chapter 9: *Joshua*.. *30*

Chapter 10: *Deborah* *32*

Chapter 11: *Samuel* *35*

Chapter 12: *Nathan* *37*

Chapter 13: *Ahijah* *39*

Chapter 14: *hemaiah* *41*

Chapter 15: *Elijah*.. *43*

Chapter 16: *Micaiah ben Imlah*.. *46*

Chapter 17: *Elisha*... *48*

Chapter 18: *Jonah* *50*

Chapter 19: *Amos* *54*

Chapter 20: *Hosea* *57*

Chapter 21: *Isaiah* *61*

Chapter 22: *Micah* *64*

Chapter 23: *Zephaniah*.. *67*

Chapter 24: *Nahum* *69*

Chapter 25: *Habakkuk* *71*

Chapter 26: *Obadiah*.. *74*

Chapter 27: *Jeremiah* *76*

Chapter 28: *Ezekiel*.. *80*

Chapter 29: *Haggai*.. *85*

Chapter 30: *Zechariah*.. *88*

Chapter 31: *Malachi*... *91*

Chapter 32: *Daniel*... *95*

Chapter 33: *John the Baptist*.. *98*

Chapter 34: *John of Revelations*.. *101*

Chapter 35: *Afterword*.. *103*

BIBLIOGRAPHY... *105*

FOREWORD

And what more shall I say? For the time would fail me to tell of Gideon and Barak and Samson and Jephthah, also of David and Samuel and the prophets: who through faith subdued kingdoms, worked righteousness, obtained promises, stopped the mouths of lions, quenched the violence of fire, escaped the edge of the sword, out of weakness were made strong, became valiant in battle ,turned to flight the armies . of aliens Women received their dead to life again. Others were tortured, not accepting deliverance, that they might obtain a better resurrection, Still others had trial of mockings and scourgings, yes, and of chains and imprisonment. They were stoned, they were sawn in two, were tempted, were slain with the sword. They wandered about in sheepskins and goatskins, being destitute ,afflicted, tormented – of whom the world was not worthy. They wandered in deserts and mountains, in dens and caves of the earth. Hebrews 11:32-38 (NKJV)

Chapter 1

What Is a Prophet?

The Biblical prophets faced many of the same harbingers of truth that the current prognosticators face today. They were ostracized, vilified, and sometimes even listened to by the public they served. Indifference of warnings can end up leading to death of cities, countries, and sometimes civilization.

Weather forecasters may announce an impending hurricane or tornado, or a fire watch may call for the evacuation of a certain area, and yet, today—just as in biblical times—there are always some who hunker down in their homes, refusing the advice of those professionals sent by a higher authority.

Farmers recognize that the productivity of a certain crop has diminished over several years. Doctors and scientist warn of an epidemic, but few believe that it could actually affect them, and a large portion of the population becomes ill. City and government inspectors try to initiate change after a catastrophe, but money and convention always win.

Today, some foretell future impending doom, or try to explain what may happen if humanity continues its current path: glaciers melt and seawaters rise, yet people are still building homes and cities in the lowlands, and next to oceans. A major earthquake fault or active volcano erupts, and people begin to rebuild before the buildings stop shaking or the lava cools.

Many Biblical prophecies have come to fruition, yet others are still in the future. Some governments, religions, or societies may work to change things, but global catastrophes and unbelief continue to shape our world, and are ignored, just as the Biblical prophets preached, alluded to, and warned.

Men tend to describe who they are by the work that they do.

Who am I? I am a student. In the past, I have been an emergency response coordinator, a welder, and a first-grade teacher. Similarly, being a prophet is a *work*, a job. Based on the lives of these biblical prophets, prophecy offered minimal payoff during their time on earth.

The word "prophet" seems to have come from the Greek "pro" meaning "before, in front of, or in place of" and "fayme" meaning "to speak". W.F. Albright suggests that the meaning of "prophet" comes from the Akkadian word "nabu" or "one who is called by God", while Konig, Lindblom, and Westermann suggest "an announcer for God"[1]. To underscore the importance of this word, "prophet" or "prophets" occurs 231 times in the Old Testament and 143 times in the New Testament. The word "prophetess" occurs 6 times in the Old Testament and 2 times in the New Testament (NIV).

The Old Testament uses four words to describe a prophet: *nãbi*, prophet; *rõ'eh*, seer; *hõzeh*, seer; and *ĩš'ĕlõhîm*, man of God. Perhaps at some time earlier, the words had separate meanings, but even in the Old Testament, the words seem to be used interchangeably.

I like Yochanan Muffs[2] example of a prophet. Both Psalm 106:23:

Therefore He said that He would destroy them,
Had not Moses His chosen one stood before Him in the breach,
To turn away His wrath, lest He destroy them. (NKJ)

and Ezekiel 22:30:

And I sought for a man among them who should build up the wall and stand in the breach before me for the land, that I should not destroy it, but I found none. (ESV)

tell of a prophet who will stand in the breach. In siege warfare, a city

---

1   www.biblestudies.com/dictionaries/prophets-prophetesses-prophesy-html
2   Muffs, Yochanan, *Who Will Stand in the Breach? A Study of Prophetic Intercession*, Cambridge, MA: Harvard University Press, 1992, p 9-48

under attack relies on the protection of its walls. Should the enemy break down or breach a section of the wall, it is up to mighty men to protect the city at the breach, its weakest point, from the attackers. It is a time of life or death and the whole city is at risk should the defenders fail. Often the prophets were placed in this situation; what they did or said often meant the life of a group of people.

Many tend to think that prophets are there to foretell the future, be a political activist, or to pave the way for the Messiah. None of these roles are as common as you might surmise. Fee and Stuart suggest that "Less than 2 percent of the Old Testament prophecy is messianic. Less than 5 percent specifically describes the new-covenant age. Less than 1 percent concerns events yet to come in our time"[3]. The bulk of the Old Testament prophet's work was to curtail sin, and warn of God's wrath to come, and to defend or advocate for the people before God, as God had declared.

All in all, most biblical prophets became intercessors for their people. They, sometimes reluctantly, ended up doing what God had told them to do. Some did that and then returned to their former occupations, some died because of their ministry (Isaiah was sawed in half), and some were just never heard from again after their prophecy. Daniel served God as a prophet for 70 years, Elijah for 52, Haggai for just 4 months. Some were princes (Daniel), priests (Jeremiah and Zechariah), and some were sheep ranchers and farmers (Amos). Some were married (Hosea), and some were told not to marry (Jeremiah). Mainly, these were just people chosen by God.

According to Deuteronomy 18:15-22, God places criteria for being a prophet:

"The LORD your God will raise up for you a Prophet like me from your midst, from your brethren. Him you shall hear, [16] according to all you desired of the LORD your God in Horeb in the day of the

3   Fee, G. and Stuart, D., *How to Read the Bible for All Its Worth*, Grand Rapids, Zondervan, 2003. P 182

assembly, saying, 'Let me not hear again the voice of the LORD my God, nor let me see this great fire anymore, lest I die.'
¹⁷ "And the LORD said to me: 'What they have spoken is good. ¹⁸ I will raise up for them a Prophet like you from among their brethren, and will put My words in His mouth, and He shall speak to them all that I command Him. ¹⁹ And it shall be that whoever will not hear My words, which He speaks in My name, I will require it of him. ²⁰ But the prophet who presumes to speak a word in My name, which I have not commanded him to speak, or who speaks in the name of other gods, that prophet shall die.' ²¹ And if you say in your heart, 'How shall we know the word which the LORD has not spoken?'— ²² when a prophet speaks in the name of the LORD, if the thing does not happen or come to pass, that is the thing which the LORD has not spoken; the prophet has spoken it presumptuously; you shall not be afraid of him. (NKJV)

The criteria are:

1) The prophet must be raised or called from the people (from your midst): Some classic examples of God's calling out prophets are in Exodus 3:10 (Moses), I Samuel 3 (Samuel), Isaiah 6 (Isaiah), Jeremiah 1 (Jeremiah), and Ezekiel 2:3 (Ezekiel).

2) God meets the prophet: God can come to the prophet, i.e., the burning bush, or in Samuel's room, or the prophet can go to God or see the normally invisible, i.e., Isaiah's and Ezekiel's visions.

3) God's Word will be placed in the prophet's mouth: The prophet is told what he or she must say and do, i.e., Moses is told to bring the Israelites out of Egypt, and Jeremiah and Isaiah are told of Israeli captivities.

4) The prophet speaks back to God:
Oftentimes, the prophet tries to extricate himself from the calling, i.e., Moses complains he is no great speaker (Exodus 4:10), or Jeremiah claims to be too young (Jeremiah 1:6).

5) God prepares the prophet for ministry, and the prophet speaks as directed: God equips the prophet, i.e., the Lord touched Jeremiah's mouth (Jeremiah 1:9), Elisha is given a cloak from Elijah (II Kings 2:13).

What does a prophet do? 1) A prophet becomes a man of God, and a servant and messenger of God. I Samuel 2:27-36 describes a man of God as one who proclaims the Word of God. This unnamed man of God prophesied to Eli of his coming woes. 2) A prophet is a custodian and sentinel for the people. Ezekiel 3:17 explains how God told Ezekiel that he was to be a watchman for Israel.

There are approximately 55 named prophets and prophetesses in the Bible, but there were literally hundreds more unnamed; for instance, the 400 prophets in I Kings 22:6 and the unnamed prophet who spoke to Eli. There were also "prophets" in other countries in the Near East. There were soothsayers and diviners in Deuteronomy 18:14; dreamers and sorcerers in Jeremiah 27:9; wise men, enchanters, and magicians in Daniel 2:27; and a medium, witch, or necromancer and spiritists found in I Samuel 28:7-14. There were casting lots and entrail reading; there were astrologers and frenzied dancing (think of Elijah on Mt. Carmel in I Kings 18:26).

Chapter 2

The God and gods of Israel and the Near East

gods

In ancient days, the people who were the most powerful, that won the skirmish or war, and who maintained the best land were seen as also having the most powerful god. Indeed, there were many gods in the Near East that caused an immense amount of havoc for the Israelites and the prophets who had to deal with Israelite "god-hopping".

In addition to national gods, there were also personal gods, household gods, city gods, and guild gods. For instance, the gods that Rachel took (stole) from her father's house were household gods (Genesis 31:19).

In Genesis 11, we find that Abram is the tenth generation of Shem, son of Noah. According to Jewish scholars,[4] Abram's father, Terach [Terah], was a maker of idols, specifically of Sin [Suen], the Chaldean Moon god, which was the main god for the city of Ur and also of Haran, where the family moved. Sin, Suen, or Nanna, are all names of this same god. He was the god associated with fertility, based on the menstrual cycle, and is pictured as a bull, most likely because the waxing moon may look like bull's horns[5].

Hadad was the god of the Amorites and later, as Adad or Rammanu, of the Akkadians and Syrians. Again, this god is portrayed as a bull and is a god of storms. His wife, Shala, is the goddess of grain. Hadad, as lord of the sky, governs rain, and thus the life of plants and growth of agriculture.

---

4   http://www.jewfaq.org/origins.htm
5   Oracc.museum.upenn.edu/amgg/listofdieties/nannasuen

The supreme god of the pantheon of gods for the Amorites and Syrians was El. Mot is the god of death and is an eater of human flesh and blood. Hadad and Mot are constantly at war[6].

Kings of the Syrians often called themselves Ben-Hadad, or son of Hadad (I Kings 20:1).

The god of the Amorites was Chemosh. King Solomon allowed this cult to be imported into Jerusalem (I Kings 11:7). The Israelite branch of the cult was destroyed by King Josiah (II Kings 23). Human sacrifices were part of the rites of Chemosh[7].

Moloch, also known as Milcom, was the god of the Ammonites. This god was usually made of bronze and had his arms held out to accept child sacrifices. A fire was placed below the outstretched arms, and small children and babies were placed into the arms as sacrifices to this god[8] (I Kings 11:7).

The Midianites, with whom Moses spent 40 years, were followers of a multitude of gods. They worshiped Ba'al, Astoroth, and Hathor[9] (Exodus 18:11).

The Egyptians worshiped many gods. Their sun god was Ra, who was also sometimes associated as a bull. Ra was considered to be self-created and made all other gods by speaking them into existence[10].

Dagon, or Dagan, was the Philistine god of fertility and grain. Sometimes he is known as a "fish-god" based on the Hebrew word "dag", meaning "fish". (Judges 16:23, I Samuel 5:1-8)[11].

Marduk was the head god of the Babylonians. The name may be derived from amar-Utu, meaning "the bull calf of the sun god Utu". He is often depicted in the form of a man accompanied by a

---

6   https://en.wikipedia/wiki/Hadad
7   www.thoughtco.com/chemosh-lord-of-the-moabites
8   https://en.wikipedia/wiki/Molech
9   https://christianity.stackexchange.com/questions/15372/what-is-the-religion-of-the-midian-people
10   https://en.wikipedia/wiki/Ra
11   https://en.wikipedia/wiki/Dagon

dragon or snake[12]. He is associated with water, vegetation, judgment, and magic[13].

In the Semitic languages of Ugaritic, Phoenician, Hebrew, Amorite, and Aramaic, the word Ba'al signified "owner" or "master". Ba'al became a word meaning "god". Originally associated with solar cults, it was eventually used for a god of storm or fertility, especially referring to Hadad[14].

Astoreth, Asteroth, Asherah, or Astarte, was the goddess of fertility, sexuality, and war[15]. She is usually pictured in a naked female form and can be traced to Sidonian, Phoenician and Canaanite beginnings. In the Bible, she is pictured as a pole, wooden image, or sacred pillar (I Kings 14:23).

God

What God did the prophets believe in, submit to, and follow? God's name is Yahweh. During the 6th to the 10th century, the Masoretes "worked to reproduce the original text of the Hebrew Bible by replacing the vowels of the name YHWH with those from the Hebrew words Adonai or Elohim. Latin speaking Christian scholars substituted the Y (which does not exist in Latin) with an I or a J."[16] The word YHWH thus became JeHoWaH, or Jehovah.

Yahweh is the name of the giver of the laws in Exodus, Leviticus, and Deuteronomy. Exodus 3:14-16 (at the burning bush) used "I AM WHO I AM" and then uses Yahweh as His name "forever" (verse 15) as the God of Abraham, Isaac, and Jacob, and the Israelite peoples.

His Name became so holy that the devout Israelites stopped writing or pronouncing it, substituting "Adonai" or Lord.

The proper meaning for Yahweh is "He Brings Into Existence

---

12   https://en.wikipedia/wiki/Marduk

13   McKenzie, John L. *Dictionary of the Bible*, Simon and Schuster, 1965 p541

14   https://en.wikipedia/wiki/Baal

15   https://en.wikipedia/wiki/Astarte

16   www.britannica.com/topic/Yahweh

Whatever Exists", or "Causes To Be". In Deuteronomy 32:6:

> *"Do you thus deal with the LORD,*
> *O foolish and unwise people?*
> *Is He not your Father, who bought you?*
> *Has He not made you and established you?"*

And in Psalm 100: 1-3:

> *"Make a joyful shout to the LORD, all you lands!*
> *² Serve the LORD with gladness;*
> *Come before His presence with singing.*
> *³ Know that the LORD, He is God;*
> *It is He who has made us, and not we ourselves;*
> *We are His people and the sheep of His pasture."*

For the prophets, God was not an abstract concept but a living God and Creator of His People. God had compassion and jealousy. God brought them out of the land of Egypt and slavery and gave them a land deeded to them forever through their father Abraham (Genesis 13:14). Genesis 34:6 proclaims that God is "merciful and gracious, longsuffering, and abounding in goodness and truth". God is compassionate, but He is also jealous.

In Exodus 20:3-5, God declares that He wants His people to have no other gods before Him, nor make any likeness of them, for He is a jealous God. Isaiah 45:14 makes the claim that there is no other God.

Yahweh had a name. He was the Creator of the universe and all that is in it. He is kind and good, and jealous in His desire to be the God of His people[17]. Here was the God of the prophets.

---

[17]   Miller, John W., *Meet The Prophets, A Beginners Guide to the Books of the Biblical Prophets*, Paulist Press, New York, 1987 p 27

Chapter 3

Abel

Abel's Life and Culture

Abel was the son of Adam and Eve, and was born after his brother, Cain. Although ousted from Eden, it seems that Adam and Eve had learned the lesson of their disobedience while living in Eden. It is likely that Abel's parents had understood that their sin required a shedding of blood after God had clothed them in animal skins, and that they passed this lesson onto their children.

While Cain became a farmer, a "tiller of ground" (Genesis 4:2), Abel became a shepherd. Since animals were usually not used for food until after the flood (Genesis 9:3), sheep were likely used for clothing and sacrifice.

Abel's Calling

We only know of Abel's calling to become a prophet from texts in the New Testament (Matthew 23:35 and Luke 11:49-51). In these verses Christ identifies Abel as a righteous prophet. It seems probable that Abel's relationship with God was such that he may have been given instructions for sacrificing animals, and on which days this was appropriate.

It is understood that people were still able to converse directly with God, as they had been able to do while in the Garden of Eden (Genesis 4:6). Genesis 4:8 tells of Abel and Cain's conversation in the fields, shortly after God's rejection of Cain's offerings. Perhaps Abel was remonstrating Cain for his decision to rebel, or encouraging him to change his ways.

Abel's Convictions

Abel communicated with God regarding his offerings. Christ Himself called Abel both righteous and a prophet. He understood the requirements for offerings and presented them humbly, not as his own works, but in recognition of God's handiwork. It appears that Abel may have been the religious leader of the family.

Abel was slain by his brother Cain during their conversation in the field (Genesis 4:8) and became the first prophet slain for his beliefs, and the first human death recorded in the Bible.

I will send them prophets and apostles,
And some of them they will kill and persecute,
That the blood of all the prophets
Which was shed from the foundation of the world
May be required of this generation,
From the blood of Abel to the blood of Zechariah....

Luke 11: 49-51

Chapter 4

Abraham

Abraham's Life and Culture

Abraham (Abram) (c. 1996-1822 B.C.[18]) was the son of Terah, or Terach. The family lived in Ur, a city traditionally placed south of Babylon. Abraham is approximately the 10th generation from Noah, in the family line of Shem. Abram had two brothers, Nahor and Haran. Haran had a son named Lot, and a daughter named Milcah, and then died. Nahor married his niece, Milcah, and Abram married his half-sister, Sarai.

According to Jewish scholars[19], Abram's father, Terah, was a maker of idols, specifically of *Sin*, the Chaldean moon god, who was the patron god of the city of Ur. Abram had many arguments with his father regarding the validity of multiple gods versus monotheism and the One True God. At one point, when his father left the shop, Abram broke all of the idols except one. He placed a hammer in the hand of the remaining idol, and when his father returned, told him that the idol had destroyed all the other idols. His father replied that it was impossible for the idol to have done that damage because the idols were not alive. Abram had made his point, but his father continued to make the idols.

At some time before Abram's 75th birthday, Terah brought Abram, Sarai, and Lot to the city of Haran, just north of Syria. They lived there, probably making idols dedicated to Sin, until Terah's death at the age of 205 (Genesis 11:32). The city of Haran was also known for its allegiance to the Chaldean god *Sin*.

---

[18]   Smith, William, *A Dictionary of the Bible*, Thomas Nelson, Nashville, 1996 p 13
[19]   http:www.jewfaq.org/origins.htm

Josephus[20] tells us that Abram left Haran because his belief in the one true God had incensed the Chaldeans, and he departed at the command and with the assistance of God. Abram was 75 when he left Haran (Genesis 12:4).

Genesis 12:1 tells of God seeking out Abram and promising him the fatherhood of a great nation and that all people on earth would be blessed through him if he would leave his country and family for a land to be shown later. Abram left Haran and traveled south toward Canaan. He stopped at Shechem, which was a sacred site to the Canaanites already living there. There was an ancient oak tree (terebinth) called "the tree of teaching". Abram camped beside it and God spoke to him again, "This land is your descendant's land". Abram built an altar to the Lord and then continued on to the mountains between Bethel and Ai, a site later known as Jerusalem. He built another altar there and called on the name of the Lord.

Abram continued southward, eventually arriving in the Negev, which means "dry" or "parched". The land was unsuitable for his animals. Having lived in a place called "the Fertile Crescent", it is likely that Abram became worried about his fate in the wasteland. Rather than trusting on God, he continued south to Egypt (Genesis 12:10). Before entering Egypt, he had instructed Sarai to present herself as his sister, fearing that her beauty might cause Pharaoh to murder him for his wife. Pharaoh did claim her, however, and took her as a concubine/wife.

God instituted a plague on Pharaoh and his house until Pharaoh questioned Abram and learned the truth of his marriage. The Pharaoh sent Abram and Sarai back to Canaan with all that they had. Abram traveled back to where he had built the altar and once more called on the Lord.

Abram was a shepherd and lived a nomadic lifestyle. Being a shepherd in Canaan required the ability to move and follow the

---

[20]   Josephus, Flavius, *The Complete Works of Josephus*, Kregel Publications, Grand Rapids, MI, 1981, p 32

grass. The immense number of sheep, oxen, donkeys, and camels required a ready supply of grass and water. A shepherd must always be ready and able to move to new pastures. Living in tents rather than permanent buildings allowed shepherds the freedom to move to new grasslands. The tents were made of goat hair and were waterproof and provided protection from the sun.

Both Abram and Lot had flocks, herds, and tents, and the land was not able to support all that they had. Abram suggested to Lot that they split the land between them. Lot chose the lush, grassy lowlands and valleys near the Dead Sea, before that land had become a desert. Abram kept his herds up in the upper valleys, foothills, and mountains.

After Lot had moved into the plain of Jordan, God spoke to Abram and told him that all he could see in every direction was his and his descendants forever (Genesis 13:14-17). Abram built an altar to the Lord near Hebron.

Five kings from the north had been taking tribute from Sodom, Gomorrah, and other neighboring lands for thirteen years. The cities revolted and refused to pay. The five kings went to war with the southern lands and conquered the whole area. They took Sodom, including Lot, his family, and all their possessions. A man who had escaped came to Abram and told him of Lot's predicament.

Abram, and his friends, the Amorites living near him, put together an army and recaptured all the goods and people that had been taken by the northern kings. When he returned, Abram was met by the King of Sodom and the King of Salem, King Melchizedek, a godly king and a priest of God. King Melchizedek gave communion and blessed Abram. Abram gave the priest-king a tithe for the Lord.

Abram returned to the King of Sodom all that he had re-captured except the food his men had eaten, and a portion for the Amorites who had helped him.

In a vision, God made a covenant with Abram, promising him an heir and descendants as numerous as the stars. God also warns

Abram of a future for his descendants that includes 400 years of oppression before Canaan will truly belong to his family.

As was customary, should a wife be unable to bear a child, a servant girl would act as surrogate and bear the child for the barren wife. Sarai was 86 years old, so she had her Egyptian servant bear her child. The boy was called Ishmael.

Abram's Calling

When Abram was 99 years old, God appeared to him. "I am almighty God; walk before me and be blameless. And I will make my covenant between Me and you and will multiply you exceedingly (Genesis 17:1-2). God then changed his name from Abram (Exalted Father) to Abraham (Father of Many). God promised him descendants and all of Canaan. God promised that He would be their God for all generations, and, as a sign of the covenant, God instituted circumcision for all males.

In his life, Abraham did not prophesy about the future. He submitted to kings and fought against kings. He was a prophet because God called him to be an intercessor.

There are two good examples of Abraham's calling. The first is his intercession for Sodom and Gomorrah. God had told Abraham in Genesis 18 that Sodom and Gomorrah would be destroyed for their wickedness. Abraham interceded for the cities in an attempt to save the righteous. This establishes Abraham as a watchman for the people.

A second instance occurs when Abraham traveled to Gerar in Genesis 20. Abraham again passed off Sarai—now Sarah—as his sister. Even at 98, Sarah must have been beautiful. The king in Gerar, Abimelech, took her into his harem. In a dream God told Abimelech that she was Abraham's wife and that he would die. King Abimelech protested, declaring his innocence and integrity. God told him to return Sarah to Abraham and to have the prophet pray for the restoration of fertility among the women in Gerar. When Sarah was returned, along with gifts of sheep, oxen, servants, and silver, Abraham interceded to God for Abimelech and his city and the city's problem was resolved.

In these two cases, only one was resolved, one was not. Sodom was not spared, but the women of Gerar were granted fertility again. Abraham was a prophet of God, not because the issues were resolved, but because he was following the dictates of his heart, and his heart was for God.

Abraham's Conviction

Abraham followed God, eventually creating a multitude of progeny. He fathered the Israelites through Isaac, the Edomites through Ishmael, and the Midianites through Midian.

Abraham doesn't perfectly fit the criteria for a prophet: he was called from his people, the Chaldeans; God spoke to him; he spoke to God, but did not complain or make excuses why he was wrong for the work; God did not tell him what to say, but Abraham did do what God told him to do; God did not equip him for any special work, but used Abraham's singular abilities of compassion and grace.

Abraham died in Canaan at 175 years of age, having followed God for 100 years.

I will make you a great nation;
I will bless you and make your name great;
And you shall be a blessing.
Genesis 12:2

Chapter 5

Moses

Moses' Life and Culture in Egypt

Moses, (c.1571-1451)[21] was the son of Amram and Jochabed, two Levites living in the land of Goshen in northern Egypt.

The family of Jacob had moved 400 years earlier[22] to Egypt as a result of a drought in Canaan and that Joseph, the next to youngest son of Jacob, had become the governor of Egypt and the Pharaoh had supplied the family of Jacob with sufficient land in northern Egypt (Goshen) for all their herds and goods (Genesis 45:17-20). +

Over the next 400 years, the family of Jacob multiplied to the extent that the Egyptians became worried that they might join Egyptian enemies to overthrow the nation (Exodus 1:10). To ensure their dominance, the Egyptians enslaved the people and forced them to build two cities, Pithom and Raameses. The cities were built with mortar and brick, made by the Hebrews.

To further ensure dominance, the Egyptians also ordered the midwives to kill every son born to Hebrew women. When that didn't work, the Hebrews were commanded "every son who is born you shall cast into the river" (Exodus 1:22).

Amram and Jochabed had a daughter named Miriam, age seven, and a son named Aaron, age three, when their third child, a boy, was born. They hid the child for three months, until they became afraid they would be discovered. Jochabed made a small vessel from bulrushes and pitch, placed the child in it, and put the vessel into the reeds of the Nile River, near where the Pharaoh's daughter bathed.

---

[21] Smith, William, *A Dictionary of the Bible*, Thomas Nelson, Nashville, 1996 p 417-418

[22] Josephus, Flavius, *The Complete Works of Josephus*, Kregel Publications, Grand Rapids, MI, 1981, p 55

The small vessel was found by Pharaoh's daughter, and the baby cried. Miriam, who had positioned herself nearby, offered to call a nursemaid for the baby. Jochabed was then commissioned to raise the child until he was weaned. After weaning, the baby was presented to the Pharaoh's daughter, who then adopted the child. She named him Moses, which means "drawn out of the water."

Moses was raised as an Egyptian prince. He would have been taught math, science, and art. He would have been instructed in religious and civil matters. He would have also been taught horseback riding and chariot warfare. He likely learned Egyptian, Akkadian, and Hebrew. Acts 7:22 explains that "Moses was learned in all the wisdom of the Egyptians and was mighty in words and deeds." Josephus devoted a chapter on General Moses' defeat of the Ethiopian attack on Egypt[23].

As Moses was one day inspecting the Hebrew workers, he witnessed an Egyptian beating a Hebrew. Offended, Moses killed the Egyptian and buried him in the sand, thinking his crime would go undiscovered. The next day, while stopping a fight between two Hebrews, one of the Hebrew men told Moses that he knew who had killed the Egyptian the day before (Exodus 2:14).

Josephus does not mention the murder of the Egyptian, but states that because of Moses' success in battle, the Egyptians were afraid of him and wanted him killed[24].

Moses, about to be killed, was about 40 years old, and fled the country, traveling east toward the Sinai Peninsula.

<u>Moses' Life in Midian</u>

The "country" of Midian was actually northeast of the Gulf of Aqaba, but there seems to be evidence that some Midianite families crossed the desert and made their way to the southern and lower

---

[23]   Josephus, Flavius, *The Complete Works of Josephus*, Kregel Publications, Grand Rapids, MI, 1981, p. 57, 58

[24]   Josephus, Flavius, The Complete Works of Josephus, Kregel Publications, Grand Rapids, MI, 1981, p 58

eastern Sinai Peninsula[25]. This is where Moses found himself. The Bible only uses one verse (Exodus 2:25) to tell how Moses went east, slipped past the series of forts placed strategically where the Suez Canal is now, and then traveled almost the length of the Sinai Peninsula, arriving near Mt Sinai, also called Mt. Horeb. Once there, he sat down near a well.

Water was precious in the desolate area and usually required great effort to obtain it. A well was dug, and water was drawn up by means of a bucket and rope. Troughs were filled to water the flocks. Often, the water drained slowly into the well and required several hours before it could be used again. Sheep and goats were often herded miles from the family or clan tents, up into the valleys, and then herded back late in the afternoon for watering and protection during the night.

The well that Moses sat near was being used by the daughters of Reuel, or Jethro, the priest of Midian. They were drawing water for the flocks of their father. Some other shepherds came with their own flocks and started to push the young women out of the way so they could water their flocks. Moses defended the women until they had watered their flocks, and was then invited to meet their father.

Moses was invited to stay and eventually married one of the daughters, Zipporah. They conceived a son and named him Gershom. Moses was put in charge of all Jethro's flocks.

Moses' Calling

Moses continued to drive the flocks to pasture. Eventually, he came to Mt. Sinai, or Horeb. It was considered to be the mountain of God. The pasturage was good there, as few people ventured onto this mountain[26]. Moses saw firelight ahead, and upon approaching

---

25   www.britannica.com/biography/Moses-Hebrew-prophet

26   Josephus, Flavius, The Complete Works of Josephus, Kregel Publications, Grand Rapids, MI, 1981, p 59

it, he noticed that a bush was burning, but not being burnt up.

God called from the fire and said, "Moses, Moses!" Moses replied, "Here I am".

God then gave Moses a set of instructions: Do not come near to this place. Take off your sandals; this is holy ground. Then God identified Himself: "I am the God of your father- the God of Abraham, the God of Isaac, the God of Jacob." Moses looked down and hid his face, afraid to look at God.

God identified the problem that needed to be fixed: "My people are being oppressed. I have heard them cry. Egypt is oppressing them. I am here to bring them out of Egypt into Canaan, a place where they can be free, a land flowing with milk and honey. To a place where Canaanites, Hittites, Amorites, Perizzites, Hivites and Jebusites live. Come, and I will send you to Pharaoh, so that you can bring My people, the children of Israel, out of Egypt."

Moses wasn't sure that God had the right Moses, "Who am I, that I should go to Pharaoh and bring out the children of Israel? Moses was probably just starting to feel at home. I'm sure he never felt comfortable either among the Egyptian elite or the downtrodden Israelites.

God said to Moses, "I will be with you, and as a sign to you, when you bring the people out of Egypt, you will meet Me here on this mountain."

Moses asked God for His name, in case the Israelites wanted to know it.

God answered him, "I AM WHO I AM," and then added, "Tell them, I AM has sent you, the Lord God of your fathers, the God of Abraham, Isaac, and Jacob has sent me. This is My name forever." (Exodus 3)

After God finished telling Moses that His people would eventually be given permission to leave, Moses asked, "What if no one listens to me, or calls me a liar?"

God then equipped Moses with a rod that could turn into a snake; the ability to cause, and remove leprosy; a mouth that could speak; and a brother as a back-up.

Moses, possibly more than any other prophet, meets the criteria for the calling of a prophet: he is called from his people; he meets with God; God tells him what to say; he speaks back to God about his unworthiness; and God equips him with tools for his ministry.

Moses' Conviction

Moses did follow God. He managed, with the use of plagues and miracles, to get the Israelites out of Egypt and headed toward Canaan. Along the way, the Israelites fell into sin, and God was going to destroy them, but Moses interceded for them (Exodus 32: 9-14; Numbers 13:11-19; Numbers 16: 20-22; Numbers 16: 44-50), clearly demonstrating his dedication to God and his people.

So, Moses led the people across the land from Egypt to Canaan - a journey of 40 years-and then died at Mt. Nebo, overlooking the Promised Land, at age 120.

For I know that after my death you will become utterly corrupt,
And turn aside from the way which I have commanded you
Deuteronomy 31:29

Chapter 6

Miriam

Miriam's Life and Culture in Egypt

Miriam, (c.1564-1452 B.C.)[27] was the daughter of Amram and Jochabed, two Levites living in the land of Goshen in northern Egypt.

The family of Jacob had moved 400 years earlier[28] to Egypt as a result of a drought in Canaan and that Joseph, the next to youngest son of Jacob, had become the governor of Egypt. Pharaoh had provided the family of Jacob with sufficient land in northern Egypt (Goshen) for all their herds and goods (Genesis 45:17-20).

During the next 400 years, the family of Jacob had multiplied to the extent that the Egyptians became worried that they might join Egyptian enemies to overthrow Egypt (Exodus 1:10). To ensure Egyptian dominance, the Egyptians enslaved the people and forced them to build two cities: Pithom and Rameses. The cities were built with mortar and brick, made by the Hebrews.

Miriam was born, according to Jewish tradition, in the same year that the Hebrew enslavement began, thus her name, meaning "bitterness". Miriam was seven years old when her brother Moses was born. Pharaoh had decreed that all male babies born to the Hebrews were to be killed (Exodus 1:22).

They hid the child for three months, until they were afraid they would be found out. Jochabed made a small vessel from bulrushes and pitch and placed the young son into it and then placed the vessel into the reeds of the Nile River, near where Pharaoh's daughter bathed.

---

[27] Smith, William, *A Dictionary of the Bible*, Thomas Nelson, Nashville, 1996 p 409

[28] Josephus, Flavius, *The Complete Works of Josephus*, Kregel Publications, Grand Rapids, MI, 1981, p 55

The small vessel was found by the Pharaoh's daughter, and the baby cried. Miriam, who had positioned herself nearby, offered to call a nursemaid for the baby. Jochabed was then commissioned to raise the child until he was weaned.

Jewish traditions tell us that Miriam was one of the chief Hebrew midwives[29].

Miriam's Calling

The Bible does not tell us of Miriam's calling to be a prophetess. However, Jewish tradition tells us that "the spirit of prophecy came to her when she was still a child. Her earliest prophecy was that her mother was would give birth to a son who would free the Jewish people from Egyptian bondage."[30]

Miriam is called a prophetess in Exodus 15:21, as she sang an affirmation of God's work in protecting the Israelites from Pharaoh's army during the exodus.

The next time she is mentioned in the Bible is when she criticizes Moses in Numbers, chapter 12. For this, she is afflicted with leprosy for seven days, until God allows her recovery and readmittance to the camp and to her position of leadership.

God gave Miriam the ability to recognize His handiwork. Other criteria for her being a prophetess can only be speculated.

Miriam's Convictions

Nothing more is heard from Miriam until her death at approximately age 127 in Kadesh. Micah, in Micah 6:4, reaffirms that God sent Moses, Aaron, and Miriam to lead the people out of Egypt.

---

[29]   www.chabad.org/library/article_cdo/aid/112396/jewish/Miriam.htm
[30]   www.chabad.org/library/article_cdo/aid/112396/jewish/Miriam.htm

"Then Miriam, the prophetess, the sister of
Aaron, Took the timbrel in her hand;
And all the women went out after her with
Timbrels and with dances."
Exodus 15:20

Chapter 7

Aaron

<u>Aaron's Life and Culture in Egypt</u>

Aaron, (c.1568-1452 B.C.)[31] was the son of Amram and Jochabed, two Levites living in the land of Goshen in northern Egypt.

The family of Jacob had moved 400 years earlier[32] to Egypt as a result of a drought in Canaan and that Joseph, the next to youngest son of Jacob, had become the governor of Egypt and Pharaoh had provided the family of Jacob with sufficient land in northern Egypt (Goshen) for all their herds and goods (Genesis 45:17-20).

During the next 400 years, the family of Jacob had multiplied to the extent that the Egyptians became worried that they might join Egypt's enemies to overthrow Egypt (Exodus 1:10). To ensure Egyptian dominance, the Egyptians enslaved the people and forced them to build two cities, Pithom and Raameses. The cities were built with mortar and bricks, made by the Hebrews.

The first mention of Aaron is in Exodus 4:14, when God tells Moses that Aaron will be his speaking voice.

<u>Aaron's Calling</u>

Aaron is called by God in Exodus 4:27 at about 83 years old (Exodus 7:7). He is told by God to meet Moses in the wilderness. He meets Moses and becomes his mouthpiece.

The criteria for being a prophet of God are satisfied. He was clearly called from among the people, God spoke to him through Moses, and he speaks for God. The Bible does not say whether Aaron tried to extricate himself from the position of prophet. In Numbers

---

31   Smith, William, *A Dictionary of the Bible*, Thomas Nelson, Nashville, 1996 p 9

32   Josephus, Flavius, *The Complete Works of Josephus*, Kregel Publications, Grand Rapids, MI, 1981, p 55

20:12 and 14 other times in the Pentateuch it is said, that the Lord spoke to Aaron.

Aaron's Conviction

In Exodus 24:9-11, Aaron saw God and had communion with Him, after serving as Moses' mouthpiece through the discourses and plagues with the Pharaoh and Egypt, and on the long journey to Mt. Sinai. In Exodus 24:14, Aaron is put in charge while Moses is on the mountain with God. Aaron is assigned as a priest by God in Exodus 28:1, and in Chapter 32, Aaron submits to the people and fabricates a golden idol. He is accused of letting the people get out of control in Exodus 32:25. In Numbers 12, both Aaron and Miriam speak against Moses and are reprimanded by God. The people, under Korah, rebel against Moses and Aaron in Numbers 16, and are punished.

Aaron follows God and Moses thereafter, and dies at the age of 122 at Mt. Hor (Numbers 20:22-29). The seeming conflict between Numbers 20 and Deuteronomy 10:6 is explained in Jewish rabbinic tradition[33]:after the war with the king of Arad, the people marched back to Mosera and then performed the mourning rites for Aaron there.

And you (Moses) shall take the anointing oil
And pour it on his (Aaron's) head,
And anoint him.
Exodus 29:7

---

33   https://en.wikipedia/wiki/Aaron

Chapter 8

Balaam

<u>Background</u>

The Amorites, sometime before the Israelites had wandered in the desert, fought with Moab, took their good land north of the Arnon River, and left the Moabites with primarily mountainous and desert lands to the south of the Arnon River.

Moses, seeking non-confrontation, asked the Israelites' kin both at Edom and Arad for safe passage through their respective countries to the land of Canaan. Both vociferously refused (Numbers 20:18, 21:1-3). The Israelites then journeyed around Moab to the Arnon River. This area was controlled by King Sihon and the Amorites.

Moses asked for permission from the Amorites to cross their lands in order to pass into Canaan. This time, King Sihon sent his army to prevent passage. Israel fought the Amorites and succeeded in defeating the Amorites. The Israelites then dwelt for some time in the cities and villages north of the Arnon River (Numbers 21:21-32).

The giant, King Og, from north of the Amorite lands, sent his army down to eliminate the Israelites but they were also defeated (Numbers 21:33-35). The Israelites then moved south to the Jordan River across from Jericho.

Balak, the son of Zippor, was the Moabite king. Fearing an Israelite invasion, he approached the elders of Edom with a proposal to counter the possible invasion by the Israelite army: they would jointly ask for the preeminent soothsayer in the land to curse the Israelites.

Balaam's Life and Culture

Balaam, son of Beor, lived in Pethor, a Syrian town south of Carchemish, along the Euphrates River. The Bible does not call him a prophet, but rather a diviner or soothsayer. Though not a progeny of Abraham, his home was very near Haran, where Abraham lived for a time.

Balaam means "devourer of the people", and his father's name means "burning"[34]. The family business seemed to involve the cursing of people or nations. Balaam was an avowed polytheist.

Balaam seemed to know of God. Perhaps he knew of God through emissaries who told of His works during the Israelites' travels, or perhaps he had heard of Abraham's witnessing 400 years earlier in Haran. In any case, it was Balaam's job to keep track of which god belonged to which tribe or nation, and which ones seemed to be stronger.

Even 400 miles from Pethor, in Moab, Balaam's reputation as one who can bless or curse a people was well known. The emissaries from Moab believed that if Balaam could weaken the Israelite God, then perhaps Balak, the Moabite army, and the Midianite army could overcome the Israelites and prevent them from taking the Moabite and Midianite land.

When asked to come and curse the Israelites, Balaam replied that he could only receive messages from the gods at night.

Balaam's Calling

While the emissaries were waiting for a reply from Balaam, God spoke to him and asked, who were those men. Balaam told God that they were men sent from Balak and wished Balaam to come and curse the Israelites.

---

[34]   www.bibletools.org/index.cfm/fuseaction/Topical.show/RTD/cgg/ID/2089/ Balaam.htm

God told Balaam that he was not to go with them or curse the Israelites. In the morning, Balaam told them that God had forbidden him to go, and they departed.

Balak sent emissaries back again, asking Balaam to come curse the Israelites. Again, Balaam told them he could only say what God told him to say. Again, God came to Balaam during the night and told him not to go unless he was asked again. Nevertheless, the next morning he saddled his donkey and left for Moab. On the way, his donkey saved him three times by recognizing the Angel of the Lord, Who had been sent to strike him down for not following God's direction. He was reminded by the Angel of the Lord to only speak God's words.

When he arrived in Moab, he told Balak that he could only speak what God told him to speak. He ended up blessing the Israelites four times, and prophesying the destruction of Amalek and the Kenites, despite Balak's displeasure.

Balaam is not called out from among the people of Israel, he is a Syrian. God did come and speak with him and told him what to say. He was a messenger of God.

Balaam's Conviction

Despite speaking with and experiencing the power of God, Balaam is not converted. He tells Balak to have his young women convince Israelite men to commit harlotry while worshiping the gods of Moab and Midian. God had to remove 24,000 Israelites before stopping the plague of evil.

Balaam was killed when the Israelites went to war against the Midianites in Numbers 31:1-8.

So he (Balaam) answered and said
"Must I not take heed to speak what the
Lord has put in my mouth?"
Numbers 22:12

Chapter 9

Joshua

Joshua's Life and Culture

Joshua, also called Hoshea (c.1530-1420 B.C.)[35] was the son of Nun, of the tribe of Ephraim.

The family of Jacob had moved 400 years earlier[36] to Egypt as a result of a drought in Canaan and that Joseph, the next to youngest son of Jacob, had become the governor of Egypt and the Pharaoh had supplied the family of Jacob with sufficient land in northern Egypt (Goshen) for all their herds and goods (Genesis 45:17-20).

During the next 400 years, the family of Jacob had multiplied to such an extent that the Egyptians became worried that they might join Egyptian enemies to overthrow Egypt (Exodus 1:10). To ensure Egyptian dominance, the Egyptians enslaved the peoples and forced them to build two cities, Pithom and Raameses. The cities were built with mortar and brick, made by the Hebrews.

The first mention of Joshua is in Exodus 17:9, when Moses assigns Joshua, then about 40 years old, as the commander of the Israelite army. In a conflict with the Amalekites. Joshua, with the help of God, defeats the Amalek army and becomes Moses' intern (Exodus 24:13).

Joshua is one of the 12 men sent to spy out the land of Canaan, and one of only two who brought back a good report (Numbers 13). Joshua and Caleb were the only two men born in Egypt who entered Canaan because "they wholly followed the Lord", (Numbers 32:12). Deuteronomy 1:38 seems to be the beginning of God's selection of the Israelite's next leader.

---

[35]   Smith, William, *A Dictionary of the Bible*, Thomas Nelson, Nashville, 1996 p 323-324

[36]   Josephus, Flavius, *The Complete Works of Josephus*, Kregel Publications, Grand Rapids, MI, 1981, p 55

Joshua's Calling

God has Moses bring Joshua into the tabernacle of meeting, so that he can be inaugurated (Deuteronomy 31:14-23). He is told to "be strong and of good courage" as he is going to be the one to bring the children of Israel into the Promised Land. Deuteronomy 34:9 tells us that Joshua was full of the spirit of wisdom, for Moses had laid hands on him.

God spoke to Joshua (Joshua 1:1-9) and is given a promise that everywhere he walked would belong to Israel and that God will be with him.

Joshua meets the criteria of a prophet in that he is called out from among the people; God speaks to him, he is told what to say and do, and God equips Joshua for his journey into Canaan. We are not told whether Joshua tried to extricate himself from the responsibility or was reluctant to obey, only that God tells him several times to be strong and of good courage.

Joshua's Conviction

Joshua continued to follow God's leading, in spite of some resistance from his own people, taking the land from the Canaanites and eventually dividing the conquered land and giving it to the tribes of Israel. As an old man, Joshua spoke to the people in Joshua 23 and 24. He reminded the Israelites to remain free of the idols and women of the Canaanite peoples. He reminded them of all God had done for them. He reminded them to serve the Lord.

In his 85 plus years, he had followed God and Moses, taken Canaan and delivered it to the people.

"But as for me and my house, we will serve the Lord".
Joshua 24:15

Chapter 10

Deborah

Background

It was about 170 years after Joshua had divided the land among the 12 tribes. Joshua had instructed the Israelites to continue clearing the land of the Canaanites and their gods. Instead, the tribes had moved into the mountains, often leaving the fertile plains to the Canaanites who were already living there.

In Judges 2:11-17 we can see the result of that:

*Then the children of Israel did evil in the sight of the L*ORD*, and served the Baals; ^{12} and they forsook the L*ORD *God of their fathers, who had brought them out of the land of Egypt; and they followed other gods from among the gods of the people who were all around them, and they bowed down to them; and they provoked the L*ORD *to anger. ^{13} They forsook the L*ORD *and served [f]Baal and the [g]Ashtoreths. ^{14} And the anger of the L*ORD *was hot against Israel. So He delivered them into the hands of plunderers who despoiled them; and He sold them into the hands of their enemies all around, so that they could no longer stand before their enemies. ^{15} Wherever they went out, the hand of the L*ORD *was against them for calamity, as the L*ORD *had said, and as the L*ORD *had sworn to them. And they were greatly distressed.*

*^{16} Nevertheless, the L*ORD *raised up judges who delivered them out of the hand of those who plundered them. ^{17} Yet they would not listen to their judges, but they played the*

harlot with other gods, and bowed down to them. They turned quickly from the way in which their fathers walked.

Othniel, Ehud, and Shamgar had delivered them from the Canaanites, but each time, after a generation, the people had returned to idolatry.

The Life and Culture of Deborah

Deborah was a prophetess and a judge who lived in the mountains of Ephraim, not too far from Shiloh, where God's tabernacle of meeting was located. She was one of a few that still worshiped Yahweh, who had given the Israelites the land.

Approximately 50 miles north of her village, Jabin, a Canaanite king, had rebuilt Hazor, and developed an army that included cavalry and 900 hundred iron armored chariots. For 20 years he had been oppressing the Israelites. His General, Sisera, was located 30 miles south and west of Hazor, where the chariots were most effective on the plains of Esdraelon at Harosheth Hagoyim, controlling the main trade routes and the richest farmland in Israel[37].

Deborah was married to Lapidoth, whose name, according to Jewish sages, meant "torches". He supplied wicks and oil to the sanctuary at Shiloh[38].

We know little of Deborah other than that she was revered in Israel. Following the general order of: 1) falling into idolatry; 2) God becomes angry and allows them to fall into oppression; 3) the Israelites cry out to God and repent; 4) God raises up a judge who delivers the people from oppression; 5) the people worship God for some time and then fall back into idolatry.

---

[37]   www.Idolphin/Deborah.html.

[38]   www.chabad.org/library/article_cdo/aid/112050/jewish/The-Prophetess-Deborah.htm

Following this cycle, evidently the Israelites were repenting and crying out for deliverance.

Deborah's Calling

Deborah was known as a prophetess (Judges 4:4) before she called Barak, so we don't know how she was called to be a prophetess.

The criteria that we know of is that she spoke for the Lord: (Judges 4:6-7)

Has not the LORD God of Israel commanded, 'Go and deploy troops at Mount Tabor; take with you ten thousand men of the sons of Naphtali and of the sons of Zebulun; ⁷ and against you I will deploy Sisera, the commander of Jabin's army, with his chariots and his multitude at the River Kishon; and I will deliver him into your hand'?

Deborah also knew that a woman would receive the glory for Sisera because Barak was reticent to lead the army for God.

Deborah's Conviction

The army of Jabin, the Canaanite king, was routed and exterminated when Barak followed God's plan and fought near the mountains, where the chariots were more ineffective, especially when God made it rain and mud bogged them down. General Sisera was killed by a woman named Jael, and Jabin lost his power over Israel.

The land had rest under Deborah's judgeship for 40 years. She became known for the song she sang, giving glory to God for the victory over the Canaanites in Judges 5.

"Nevertheless there will be no glory for you
In the journey you are taking,
For the Lord will sell Sisera into the hand of a woman."
Judges 4:9

Chapter 11

Samuel

<u>Samuel's Life and Culture</u>

Samuel (c.1171 B.C.)[39] was the son of Elkanah, a Levite, and Hannah, and was born in Ramathaim Zophim, in the mountains of Ephraim. As was not uncommon at the time, Elkanah was the husband of two wives: Penninah was able to bear children, Hannah seemed to be barren. Being barren was a huge disappointment: see Sarah and Abraham (Isaac), Jacob and Rachel (Joseph), Manoah and his wife (Samson), Zacharias and Elisabeth (John the Baptist).

Israel had recently gone to war against their own: the tribe of Benjamin (Judges 19-21). The Philistines, the Ammonites, and the Edomites were constantly pressuring their neighboring tribes of Israelites. Samson, the last judge of Israel, had been killed, and many of the Israelites were worshiping false gods. Eli was the priest at Shiloh, at the tabernacle of God.

Hannah came and prayed at the temple, vowing that if she were to bear a son, he would belong to the Lord as a Nazarite. Eli observed her, questioned her, and then told her that the Lord would grant her request. Samuel was born, and after being weaned, he was given to Eli to raise in the priesthood at Shiloh.

<u>Samuel's Calling</u>

Samuel was now living with Eli. He had been acting as a junior priest from the time he could walk until he was 12 years old[40]. One

---

[39]   Smith, William, *A Dictionary of the Bible*, Thomas Nelson, Nashville, 1996, p 586

[40]   Josephus, Flavius, *The Complete Works of Josephus*, Kregel Publications, Grand Rapids, MI, 1981, p 122

evening, as Samuel was almost asleep, God called him by name. Samuel thought that Eli had called him and went to him. Eli replied that he had not called him and told him to return to bed.

God called Samuel by name again, and again Samuel assumed that Eli had called him, and again he was sent back to bed.

Again, God called Samuel by name, and Samuel went to Eli. This time Eli suspected that it was God who had spoken to Samuel and instructed him to answer, "Speak, Lord, for your servant hears."

God called Samuel yet again, and this time Samuel understood and answered as Eli had directed him. The Lord told Samuel what was to happen to Eli and his sons.

In the morning, Eli asked Samuel what the Lord had said, and Samuel related it to him.

The book of I Samuel, chapter 3: 19-21 relates that Samuel, from that point on, was recognized by all of Israel as a prophet of the Lord.

Samuel follows the criteria for a prophet in that he was called from among the people, and God came and spoke to him. He was told what to say and do by God.

Samuel's Conviction

Samuel judged Israel until his death (I Samuel 7:15). He, under God's direction, anointed first Saul, and then David as kings of Israel. He was known as a seer, priest, judge, prophet, and military leader[41]. He is believed to have led a band of prophets that roamed the country.

I Samuel 25:1 tells of his death and burial at Ramah.

But Samuel ministered before the Lord
Even as a child.
I Samuel 2:18

---

[41]   www.britannica.com/biography/Samuel-Hebrew-prophet

Chapter 12

Nathan

Nathan's Life and Culture

Nathan (c. 1015 B.C.)[42] was the son of Attai (I Chronicles 2:36). His grandfather was an Egyptian named Jarha, and Attai's mother was of the tribe of Judah. Nathan was born during the time of Samuel. His son Zabad is said to have been a friend of David[43].

Nathan's Calling

There is no biblical record of Nathan's calling. It is speculated that Nathan may have been one of Samuel's band of traveling prophets (I Samuel 19:20).

His first mention, in II Samuel 7:2, refers to him as Nathan the prophet. He is asked by David if it is permissible to build a house for the Ark of the Covenant. Nathan, thinking it is a great idea, affirms the plan. That night, the word of the Lord came to Nathan. God told him that He did not desire a house, but that David's family would become a house for all generations. Verse 14 indicates the Son of God would also come from this family.

Nathan follows the criteria of a prophet in that he speaks what he is told by God.

---

[42] Smith, William, *A Dictionary of the Bible*, Thomas Nelson, Nashville, 1996, p 433

[43] Bible.wikia.com/wiki/Nathan_(Prophet)

Nathan's Conviction

Nathan continues as a "court prophet", and in II Samuel 12, confronts David with the word of the Lord regarding his sin with Bathsheba and Uriah. He then prophesies that David would not die, but that his son by Bathsheba would die (II Samuel 12:14).

Later, he would ensure that Solomon would ascend the throne (I Kings 1); and likely wrote a chronology called the "*Book of Nathan the Prophet*", mentioned in I Chronicles 29:29 and II Chronicles 9:29.

> *Then Nathan said to David,*
> *"You are the man!*
> *Thus says the Lord God of Israel:*
> *I anointed you king over Israel,*
> *And I delivered you from the hand of Saul"*
> *II Samuel 12:7*

Chapter 13

Ahijah

Background

Solomon, son of David, was the king of Israel. He had been king for just under 40 years. During his reign, the Ark was moved into a Temple in Jerusalem (I Kings 8). Solomon accumulated much wealth, chariots, and horses (I Kings 10: 23, 26), and 700 wives and 300 concubines (I Kings 11:3). Many of his wives had also brought their own gods, which eventually caused Solomon to turn away from God. He began to worship the gods Ashtoreth, Chemosh, Molech, Milcom, and others. The Lord God became angry (I Kings 11:9).

Ahijah's Life and Culture

Ahijah (c.956 B.C.)[44] lived in Shiloh. We only know that he was older (I Kings 14:4).

Ahijah's Calling

He is first mentioned as a prophet in I Kings 11:29. He found one of Solomon's mighty men of valor, Jeroboam; a man who had been put in charge of repairing the defensive walls and towers of Jerusalem. Ahijah spoke the words of the Lord to Jeroboam, telling him he was to become king of the northern ten tribes, while Solomon's family would retain Judah. He also warned Jeroboam that he should walk in the ways of the Lord or face the same consequences that David's family faced.

---

[44] Smith, William, *A Dictionary of the Bible*, Thomas Nelson, Nashville, 1996, p 26

Ahijah's Convictions

Ahijah is mentioned again in I Kings 14:1-17, when he is told by the Lord that Jeroboam's son would die because of the evil that Jeroboam had done by appointing priests from any tribe, establishing shrines in high places, manufacturing idols, personally offering sacrifices, and worshiping evil gods. Israel was to be given up, and the Israelites scattered.

And he (Ahijah) said to Jeroboam,
"Take for yourself ten pieces,
For thus says the Lord, the God of Israel:
Behold, I will tear the kingdom out of the hand of Solomon
And will give ten tribes to you."
I Kings 11:31

Chapter 14

Shemaiah

Background

Solomon died after a 40-year reign (c.1015-975 B.C.) and his son, Rehoboam, became king. After taking poor advice from friends and exacting onerous taxes from the people, Jeroboam, one of Rehoboam's servants and a man of valor, was instructed by God through the prophet Abijah to take the upper ten tribes and secede from Rehoboam.

Shemaiah's Life and Culture

Shemaiah (c.972 B.C.)[45] was the court prophet and chronicler for King Rehoboam (II Chronicles 12:15). He is first mentioned in I Kings 12:22 and was called a "man of God" and a prophet in II Chronicles 12:5.

Shemaiah's Calling

We know nothing of Shemaiah's calling, only that he spoke for the Lord.

Shemaiah's Convictions

In the first year of King Rehoboam's reign, God told Shemaiah to tell the King to cease planning for war with Israel to the north. In the fifth year of Rehoboam's reign, the pharaoh of Egypt, Shishak,

---

[45]   Smith, William, *A Dictionary of the Bible*, Thomas Nelson, Nashville, 1996, p 616

attacked Jerusalem. Shemaiah told King Rehoboam that he was to be left in the hands of the Egyptians because he had forsaken God.

"But the word of God came to Shemaiah
The man of God."
I Kings 12:22

Chapter 15

Elijah

Background

In the northern country of Israel, Jeroboam (ruled c.922-901 B.C.) died, leaving the throne to his son, Nadab (ruled 901-900 B.C.) who was then assassinated by Baasha (ruled c.900-877 B.C.)[46], who ascended to the throne of Israel. All were wicked in that they worshiped false gods. Elah, son of Baasha, succeeded Baasha after 22 years. After 2 years, Elah was assassinated by Zimri, commander of the Israelite chariots (I Kings 16:9).

After seven days, Zimri committed suicide after Israel made Omri king. Omri (c.876-869 B.C.) moved the capital of Israel to a city he built called Samaria (I Kings 16:24). After twelve years, Omri died, leaving the throne to his son, Ahab.

Ahab married the princess of Sidon, the daughter of the king, Ethbaal. The Sidonians were Phoenicians and worshiped both Baal and Asherah. Jezebel brought her gods and the priests of those gods with her to Samaria. Ahab embraced those gods and built altars and temples to them.

Elijah's Life and Culture

Elijah was from Thesbon in Gilead[47], and was called a Tishbite (I Kings 17:1). Gilead was a rocky, mountainous area inhabited originally by Amorites and at the time of Elijah, by the tribe of

---

46   Leclerc, Thomas L., *Introduction to the Prophets*, Paulist Press, New York, 2017, p 87

47   Josephus, Flavius, *The Complete Works of Josephus*, Kregel Publications, Grand Rapids, MI, 1981, p 190

Manasseh, who used the valleys and mountain slopes primarily for grazing goats and sheep.

Elijah's name means *My God is Jehovah.* He was usually dressed in a girdle of skin and wore a mantle, or cape, made of sheepskin.

Elijah's Calling

We know nothing of Elijah's calling, only that he suddenly appeared at King Ahab's palace in Samaria, declaring that a drought was to be initiated at the command of God. God had declared war on the concept of both Baal, the god of rain, lightning, and thunder, and on Asherah, the goddess of fertility. God then told Elijah to go hide near the Brook Cherith, where he was to be fed by ravens.

Elijah met the criteria of a prophet in that God told Elijah what to do, and then equipped him for the task.

Elijah's Convictions

Elijah is fed by the ravens until even the mountain brooks run dry. He is then sent to the heart of Sidonian country, Zerephath, where he feeds a widow and her son, and himself, from a never-ending bin of flour and a never-ending jar of oil for the remainder of the three and a half years of drought, he also performs another miracle; reviving the widow's son, who had become sick and died.

After about three and a half years of drought throughout Israel, Sidonia, and Syria, Elijah finds Obadiah, Ahab's servant, and asks to meet with the king. Obadiah arranges a meeting, and Elijah accuses Ahab of following the Baals and forsaking the commandments of God. Elijah tells Ahab to bring the children of Israel and all 850 prophets of Baal and Asherah to the top of Mt. Carmel.

First, Elijah challenges the people to follow God and allows the prophets of Baal to prepare a sacrifice to Baal, but to allow only

Baal to light the sacrifice with fire. The prophets worked all day to get the fire started but were unsuccessful.

Elijah built an altar and laid the sacrifice on it and then poured water over it. He then called on God to light the fire. The fire was so hot that even the stones of the altar were consumed. Thus, the people understood that there was only one true God. The people seized the false prophets and all 850 prophets were executed. Shortly thereafter rain came to the country (I Kings 18:45).

Jezebel was angry that her prophets had been executed and threatened Elijah with the same. He was given provisions by God and escaped to Mount Horeb. There, he spoke with God and is given instructions to anoint a new king over Syria and a new king over Israel and then he was to anoint a prophet to replace himself: Elisha.

Elijah first secured his replacement but did not anoint the kings as God had instructed. II Kings 2:1-11 tells of Elijah's miraculous entry into heaven by way of a fiery chariot.

Then you call on the name of your gods,
And I will call on the name of the lord;
And the God who answers by fire,
He is God.
I Kings 18:24

Chapter 16

Micaiah ben Imlah

<u>Background</u>

King Ahab of Israel continued in his evil, worshiping the gods of the Canaanites and Sidonians. Israel, the northern kingdom, had been at war with Syria for some time. Israel had defeated the Syrians in the last two battles (I Kings 20). A treaty between the two antagonists was in effect when King Ahab asked King Jehoshaphat of Judah to help him in retrieving cities in Gilead from the Syrians. King Jehoshaphat asked for a prophet to inquire of the Lord to allay his fears of defeat. Ahab's prophets, especially Zedekiah the son of Chenaanah, all declared that the Lord said that Israel would prevail in the war.

King Jehoshaphat requested that a prophet of the Lord be summoned. Ahab then requested that Micaiah ben Imlah be found and asked. He also stated that this prophet of God had previously prophesied negatively against Ahab.

<u>Micaiah ben Imlah's Life and Culture</u>

It is possible that Micaiah was the "man of God" in I Kings 20:28 and 20:35-43, but it is not certain. In II Chronicles 17:7 a Micaiah, described as a leader, was sent to teach the Book of the Law in Judah by King Jehoshaphat.

<u>Micaiah's Calling</u>

We know only that Micaiah spoke the words of the Lord.

Micaiah's Convictions

When the messenger suggested that Micaiah tell King Ahab the same thing other prophets were saying, he replied that he would only speak what the Lord told him (I Kings 22:14).

Micaiah ben Imlah approached the two kings and was asked if Israel and Judah should go to war against Syria. The prophet replied that the king will win, but he did not specify which king. When confronted by Ahab, Micaiah told the kings and prophets of his vision of heaven, in which the Lord allowed a spirit to send a lying message through the prophets.

Zedekiah, the false prophet, then slaps Micaiah and Ahab ordered him to be sent to prison with bread and water until he returned from the battle with Syria.

Micaiah tells King Ahab that he will not be returning from the battle alive. As prophesied, Ahab is killed in battle (I Kings 22:35), proving that Micaiah and not Zedekiah was the true prophet.

"There is still one man, Micaiah the son of Imlah,
By whom we may inquire of the Lord;
But I hate him, because he does not
prophesy good concerning me,
But evil."
I Kings 22:8

Chapter 17

Elisha

Elisha's Life and Culture

Elisha (c.850-798) was the son of Shaphat from Abel-meholah. Abel-meholah was in the Jordan valley near the Jordan River, either in East Issachar or West Manasseh[48]. He was a farmer, plowing a field with twelve yoke of oxen when Elijah approached him.

King Ahab was the king of Israel, at war with the Syrians, and had been sentenced to death by God through Elijah's prophecies.

Elisha's Calling

Elisha said goodbye to his father and mother, sacrificed two oxen for a farewell dinner, and left with Elijah. He follows the criteria to be a prophet in that he was called from the people, he was equipped by God, and he spoke what God directed him to speak.

Elisha is called by God to be a prophet when Elijah threw his mantle of sheepskin on his shoulders (I Kings 19:19). Throwing his mantle over Elisha signified his investiture as a prophet and of his adoption as a son of Elijah[49].

Elisha's Convictions

Elisha follows Elijah for eight years, until Elijah is taken to heaven by a chariot of fire. He then picks up Elijah's sheepskin mantle, takes on the spirit of Elijah, and parts the Jordan River

---

48 https://bibleatlas/abel-meholah/htm

49 Smith, William, A Dictionary of the Bible, Thomas Nelson, Nashville, 1996, p 167

(II Kings 2:14), purifies the spring water in Jericho (II Kings 2:21), curses young men who verbally assaulted him (II Kings 2:24), and provides water for the coalition of Israel, Judah, and Edom who were attacking Moab, and prophesies that the coalition would be victorious (II Kings 3). Later he miraculously supplies oil to a grieving widow (II Kings 4: 1-7), raised a Shunammite's son from the dead (II Kings 4:8-37), cleansed a pot of poisonous stew (II Kings 4:38-41), fed one hundred men with twenty small loaves of bread (II Kings 4:42-44), and healed Naaman, the leprous commander of the Syrian army (II Kings 5:1-19).

He prophetically caught his servant, Gehazi, stealing (II Kings 5:20-27), floated an iron ax head from the water (II Kings 6:1-7), blinded the eyes of the Syrian army (II Kings 6:8-23), prophesied of a seven-year famine (II Kings 8:1), predicted that Hazael would reign over Syria after assassinating King Ben-Hadad (II Kings 8:7-15), had Jehu anointed as king of Israel (II Kings 9:1-13), and prophesied of Syria's defeat on his deathbed (II Kings 13:14-19).

Elisha died (II Kings 13:20), but even after he was entombed, his bones were touched by a dead man, who revived.

Elisha said, "Please let a double portion of your spirit
Be upon me."
II Kings 2:9

Chapter 18

Jonah

Background

In c. 762 BC, Jeroboam II was king of Israel, the northern ten tribes. King Jeroboam had also taken as allies or vassal states the countries of Syria, Phoenicia, Philistia, Edom, Ammon, and Moab[50]. Their country was as large as it had ever been, even when King Solomon had expanded Israel.

Assyria, which had just years before more or less dominated Israel, was at war with their northern neighbor, Uratu, and had temporarily ceased harassing Syria and Israel.

In the past Shalmaneser III[51] in c.841 B.C. and Ashur-Dan III in c.772 B.C. had attacked Damascus and Israel. Israel had been paying tribute since the reign of King Jehu of Israel.

The Assyrians were known for their cruelty to those who lost a war with them. Captives were placed on stakes and hanged, children were burnt to death, and heads were hung on trees around the captured cities[52].

The current King of Assyria, Ashur-dan III was battling against revolts from conquered nations. In c. 765 B.C. and in c.759 B.C. Assyria was experiencing plagues. In c.760 B.C. an earthquake of immense proportion struck the area. The country of Uratu was

---

[50]   Leclerc, Thomas L., *Introduction to the Prophets*, Paulist Press, New York, 2017, p 118

[51]   https://en.wikipedia.org/wiki/Shalmaneser_III

[52]   Fuhr, Richard Alan and Yates, and Yates, Gary E., The Message of the Twelve: Hearing the Voice of the Minor Prophets, B&H Academic, Nashville, 2016 p 163

attacking the northern borders of Assyria. Assyria was questioning its god, Adad.

While Ashur was the capital of Assyria, Nineveh was an old city, built just after the flood (Genesis 10:8-12). It was not just a city, but a region of cities and farmland, extending about 60 miles in circumference.

Jonah's Life and Culture

II Kings 14:23-25 states that Jonah, son of Amatai, was a prophet who had prophesied that King Jeroboam II would restore the boundaries of Israel. Jeroboam extended Israel to about Solomon's size two centuries earlier.

We know nothing of Jonah's previous life except that he was from Gath-Hepher, a city about four miles northeast of what was to be Nazareth, in Galilee[53].

Israel was experiencing economic growth; the trade route from Egypt to Assyria and Babylon passed through Israel and prosperity was apparent, with opulent homes being built for the rich.

Jonah's Calling

We do not know Jonah's original calling to be a prophet. The first calling mentioned in the Bible is in Jonah 1:1. God spoke to Jonah and told him to go to Nineveh and preach against it because of its wickedness. Moses and Jeremiah both thought themselves unable to do as God asked. Jonah did not say no or argue with God; he traveled down to Joppa and boarded a merchant vessel heading as far away from Nineveh as possible at that time: to a city called Tarshish in southern Spain.

---

[53]   Hailey, Homer, *A Commentary on the Minor Prophets*, Baker Book House, Grand Rapids Michigan, 1972, p 62

A storm arose, and the sailors were in fear of their lives. They cast lots, and Jonah's name came up. He admitted that he was running away from God and told them that, were they to cast him overboard the sea would calm and they would be safe. Eventually they threw him overboard and the sea calmed.

God provided a great fish to swallow Jonah. He was inside the fish for three days and nights. Chapter 2 tells of Jonah's prayer, which includes both thanksgiving and praise.

In Chapter 3, God again calls Jonah to go to Nineveh and proclaim God's message. Jonah 3:3 tells us that he obeyed the word of the Lord and traveled to Nineveh.

Jonah follows the criteria of being a prophet because God calls him; he is told what to do, and he does it, in spite of attempting to extricate himself from the responsibility.

Jonah's Convictions

On the first day Jonah arrived in Nineveh, he began to proclaim, "Forty more days and Nineveh will be overturned." Within the previous five years (approximately) there had been two plagues, an earthquake, and revolts. The people were ready for a change. The Ninevites believed God and repented. The king then demanded that all inhabitants of the city fast and call on God for mercy and repentance (Jonah 3:7-9).

Jonah 3:10 explains that their repentance moved God to show mercy, and He relented from the destruction He had threatened.

Chapter 4 begins with Jonah's displeasure at the cessation of punishment for the inhabitants of Nineveh. Jonah explained to God that the reason he had run from this assignment was that he knew God was merciful and compassionate, and that he was afraid that the wicked Ninevites might not receive the punishment Jonah believed they so rightly deserved. In Jonah's anger and frustration, he asks God to take his life. God tells Jonah that he has no right to be angry.

Jonah sits outside the city and builds himself a shelter from the sun. That night, God causes a vine to grow over the shelter for shade. Jonah is appreciative of the vine. The next morning, God provides a worm to chew the vine, which withers. With the vine withered, Jonah loses his shade. God then sends a hot wind toward Jonah, and again Jonah wants to die.

God chastised Jonah for worrying about the vine instead of the 120,000 Ninevites.

I knew that you were a gracious and compassionate God,
Slow to anger and abounding in love,
A God who relents from sending calamity.
Jonah 4:2

Chapter 19

Amos

Background

Around c. 762 B.C. Jeroboam II was king of Israel, the northern ten tribes, while Uzziah was the king of Judah. A generation before, Uzziah's father, King Amaziah, had initiated a war with King Joash of Israel and was defeated. The two current kings of Judah and Israel, however, were using this period of peace to strengthen their borders.

King Jeroboam II had also taken as allies or vassal states the countries of Syria, Phoenicia, Philistia, Edom, Ammon, and Moab[54]. He controlled the main trade route from Egypt to the Tigris River. The Israelites, through trade, were experiencing economic prosperity. Their country was as large as it had ever been, even during King Solomon's expansion of Israel. Many rich families were building both summer and winter homes, complete with fine furniture and ivory paneling, on land taken from or purchased from poor farmers, who were then relegated as to tenant farmers, essentially slaves.

The rich were treating those not endowed with wealth very poorly and unjustly. Many judges were corrupt, and people were worshiping the golden calves introduced by Jeroboam I.

Assyrian, which had only years before more or less dominated Israel, was now at war on its northern borders with Uratu and had temporarily ceased harassing Syria and Israel.

The earthquake mentioned in Amos 1:1 occurred around 760 B.C. and must have been horrific (Amos 6:11, 9:5)[55]. Amos predicted the earthquake two years before it occurred.

---

[54] Leclerc, Thomas L., *Introduction to the Prophets*, Paulist Press, New York, 2017, p 118

[55] Yadin, Yilgal, *Hazor II: An Account of the Second Season of Excavations*, Magnes Press, Jerusalem, 1956

Amos' Life and Culture

In Amos 1:1 we find that Amos was a sheep breeder (NKJV) and lived in Tekoa. The "nakads" sheep he bred were of a very small size but were known for their proclivity and quality of wool[56].

Tekoa was a village about twelve miles south and east of Jerusalem in Judah. Because of its height and strategic location, the mountaintop had been used as a watchtower for generations[57]. The area was rugged and mountainous, about eighteen miles west of the Dead Sea. In the steep valleys and canyons where the sheep grazed, there were lions and jackals.

In Amos 7:14 we also learn that he was a farmer who tended sycamore trees. This sycamore was a type of fig tree that required each fruit to be scratched or bruised while on the tree in order to ripen. These trees grew in the Jordan Valley, about 2,800 feet in elevation below the village of Tekoa.

King Uzziah was king of Judah (c.793-753 B.C.) and due to peace and urbanization, with the rich becoming richer and the poor becoming poorer, both Judah and Israel faced an explosive situation[58].

Amos' Calling

In Amos 7:14-15 we see Amos' call to be a prophet. He was out with his sheep, following his flock as they moved from meadow to meadow. The Lord "took" him and told him to "Go, and prophesy to My people Israel". He was sent as a missionary prophet to a country that spoke essentially the same language, but to a people completely different. He was sent to speak to rich, indolent people of little morality or work ethic, while he had worked his entire life.

---

[56]   Hailey, Homer, *A Commentary on the Minor Prophets*, Baker Book House, Grand Rapids Michigan, 1972, p 82

[57]   Miller, John W., *Meet the Prophets*, Paulist Press, New York, 1987, p 44, 45

[58]   Leclerc, Thomas L., *Introduction to the Prophets*, Paulist Press, New York, 2017, p 120, 121

Amos follows the criteria for being a prophet in that he is called from among the people; God speaks to him; he speaks what God tells him to speak. Some argument can be made that God also equipped Amos by his upbringing and occupation.

Amos' Convictions

Amos begins his ministry just north of Jerusalem, in Bethel, Israel. Bethel was one of two places of worship in the northern kingdom established by Jeroboam I to prevent worship in Jerusalem (I Kings 12:28-29).

He begins by proclaiming God's judgment against Syria (Amos 1:3-5); the Philistines (1:6-8); Tyre (1:9-10); Edom (1:11-12); Ammon (1:13-15); Moab (2:1-3); Judah (2:4-5); and Israel (3:6-4:15). He pulls no punches; the surrounding countries are to be invaded by fire for their warlike posture and atrocities against each other and against Judah and Israel.

Judah and Israel will be taken captive because of their crimes against each other (Amos 2:6-8), their loss of compassion for the poor and their loss of integrity (Amos 6:12).

Amos follows his condemnations with visions. The first two visions of a locust plague and a consuming fire were averted by God at Amos' behest. The last three; of Israel's destruction God does not avert.

Amos completes his proclamations with the restoration of Israel; the return of the captives, the rebuilding of the tabernacle (Amos 9:11-15).

> *"I will plant them in their land,*
> *And no longer shall they be pulled up*
> *From the land I have given them,"*
> *Says the Lord your God."*
> *Amos 9:1*

Chapter 20

Hosea

Background

Life was relatively peaceful and profitable during the reign of Jeroboam II, until his death (died c.746 B.C.)[59]. After his death (II Kings 14:29) his son, Zechariah reigned for six months until Shallum ben Jabesh assassinated him and became king of Israel. Shallum was king for just one month and was assassinated by Menahem, who took the crown. In c.743 B.C., Tiglath-pileser III (Pul, NKJV) of Assyria subdued Israel and forced a heavy tribute on the land (II Kings 15:19,20). The richer people of Israel began exploiting and cheating the poor in order to pay the tax (Hosea 12:7,8). After approximately 8 years, Menahem died and was succeeded by his son, Pekahiah (II Kings 15:23) who reigned for two years before being assassinated by Pekah ben Remaliah (c. 736 B.C.).

King Pekah joined with Syria and the Philistines and attempted to force Judah to join them against Assyria. Around 732 B.C. King Pekah was assassinated by Hoshea bar Elah, who then rules as King of Israel. Judah sought assistance from Assyria, which then annexed the northern lands of Naphtali, Gilead, and Galilee, and dispersed that population into Assyria.

Upon the death of Tiglath-pilezer III (around 727 B.C.), King Hoshea allied with Egypt and refused to pay tribute to Assyria under its new king, Shalmaneser V, and in c.725 B.C., began a three-year siege of Samaria. Upon Shalmaneser's death, Sargon II continued the siege and eventually took 27,290 Israelites to Assyria, bringing

---

[59] Leclerc, Thomas L., *Introduction to the Prophets*, Paulist Press, New York, 2017, p 147

an end to the country of Israel (c. 722 B.C.[60]). Assyria them imported peoples from Babylon, Cuthah, Ava, Hamath, and Sepharvaim (II Kings 17:24).

Throughout this period, the Israelites continued to worship both the Baals and the two golden calves established by King Jeroboam, completely forgetting their covenant with God.

Hosea's Life and Culture

We know little of Hosea's life before his calling. He was the son of Beeri. Hans Wolffe[61] suggests that he was a member of the Levitical priesthood. Others (LeClerc, Hailey) suggest he may have been a farmer based on Hosea 3:2 and his redemption of Gomer for silver and barley.

Most scholars place his home in Samaria, making him the only writing prophet from the north, in Israel.

Hosea's Calling

Hosea's calling is found in the first chapter. God spoke to him and told him to find a wife, not just any wife, but a wife of "harlotry". John Miller, in *Meet the Prophets*, suggests that she was not a whore, or harlot, as we think of them, but one who had sexual relations at a place of worship at a Canaanite shrine. God explained that this was to represent the land (people of Israel) and their proclivity for idol worship. Verse three tells us that he took Gomer, daughter of Diblain, as wife.

His second encounter with God was after they conceived a child. God told him that the boy was to be named Jezreel, meaning "God will scatter, or God will sow" (Hosea 1:4).

---

60   Fuhr, Jr.,Richard Alan and Yates, Gary E.. *The Message of the Twelve*, B & H Academic, Nashville, Tennessee, 2016, p 60

61   Wolff, Hans Walter, Hosea, Hermeneia , Fortress Philadelphia, 1974

Jezreel has many implications: It was the place where Jehu killed Ahab's family, became king, and then followed the Baals just as his predecessors had done (II Kings 9:7-10:31). Jehu's descendant, King Zechariah, was assassinated at Jezreel by Shallum (II Kings 15:10). In Hosea 1:5 it states that the Valley of Jezreel is where the end of Israel would take place. In c. 722 B.C. Assyria conquered Israel in the Valley of Jezreel and scattered her people among the Assyrian Empire.

Gomer conceived again and bore a daughter. God told Hosea that she was to be named Lo-Ruhammah, meaning "No mercy, No pity, No compassion, Not loved". God explained to Hosea that He would no longer be merciful to Israel, but that He would extend mercy to Judah by His power (Hosea 1:6,7 and Isaiah 37:36-37).

After Lo-Ruhammah is weaned, Gomer conceives again. God tells Hosea that this boy is to be named Lo-Ammi, which means "Not My People" and then He tells Hosea that He has rejected Israel as their God (Hosea 1:9).

God continues by telling Hosea that in the future (see Ezekiel 36 and 37) the people will be restored as "sons of the living God" (Hosea 1:10, 11).

Hosea's Convictions

Hosea, beginning in chapter 2:2 begins his mission to the people. He relates, as God tells him, that Israel and Judah are just like Hosea's marriage. The people have committed whoredom by worshiping gods other than the God who brought them out of Egypt. God is divorcing His wife, the people of Israel. The land is to become bare: there will be no grain, no crops of wine or olives or figs, and no herds. The only thing growing will be thistles.

In Hosea 2:14, God then tells Hosea to relate to the people that He will restore the people once they remember their God, and He will restore the land.

Chapter 3 tells of Hosea having to redeem his wife, who had returned to her previous life. He purchases her for silver and barley (Hosea 3:2), but they are to remain chaste, demonstrating Israel's loss of God and kings because of their idolatry and immorality.

Chapter 4:15 warns Judah that following the path of Israel would result in similar circumstances.

Chapter 6 is God's call to repentance, but it is futile (Hosea 7:14). Chapter 9:3 tells of the people being taken to Assyria, in spite of their reliance on Egypt.

Chapter 14 ends the book of Hosea with a promise of restoration after repentance.

"I will heal their backsliding,
I will love them freely,
For My anger has turned away from him."
(Hosea 14:4)

Chapter 21

Isaiah

Background:

LeClerc, Miller, and other scholars maintain that the Book of Isaiah was probably written by three different authors at different times and then collated into the Book of Isaiah. These scholars refer to Isaiah, the son of Amoz, as the author of chapters 1-39 because this materials reflect events that happened during the lifetime of Isaiah and was written from the perspective of someone living in Jerusalem. This part the scholars call "Proto-Isaiah". The period of these writings dates to c. 740-700 B.C.

Scholars attribute chapters 40-55 to "Deutero-Isaiah", which takes place 200 years later after the first wave of Persian conquests and is written from the perspective of someone living in Babylon. These chapters date to c. 546-538 B.C.

These scholars refer to the author of chapters 56-66 as "Trito-Isaiah". These passages are written from the perspective of a Jerusalem wasteland prior to the rebuilding of the temple in c. 515 B.C. These chapters date to c. 537-520 B.C.

These scholars agree that Isaiah son of Amoz could not have named Cyrus 200 years before the ruler came to power in Babylonia.

Contrary to these scholars, and in agreement with Thomas Nelson's NKJV Study Bible, I believe God is all-knowing of the future and will continue this chapter as if Isaiah were a single entity and the author of the Book of Isaiah.

The Life and Culture of Isaiah bar Amoz.

Miller[62] asserts that Isaiah was probably a court prophet or teacher with disciples.

LeClerc[63] suggests he might have come from a courtroom background based on his language of indictments and prosecutions to the kings he served.

Isaiah prophesied from c. 742 B.C. until his death at age 90[64]. All writings by Isaiah indicate that he lived in Jerusalem, though he never stated his residence.

Isaiah lived during the reigns of Kings Uzziah, Jotham, Ahaz, and Hezekiah (Isaiah 1:1). He was married to a prophetess (Isaiah 8:3) and had two sons.

Jewish tradition has King Manasseh sentencing Isaiah to death by being sawn in half at age 90.

Isaiah's Calling

Isaiah has one of the most extensive writings on his calling to be a prophet in Isaiah chapter 6. We know the year: c. 742 B.C., the year that King Uzziah died and his son Jotham began his reign.

In a vision, Isaiah is brought to the throne of God. He sees seraphim with six wings calling out "Holy, holy, holy is the Lord of Hosts." Isaiah feels so unholy in the presence of God that he cries out that he is undone, for he is a man of unclean lips. A seraphim flies over with a live coal from the altar of God and touches Isaiah's mouth, taking away his iniquity (Isaiah 6:1-7), and making his speech pure for God's words.

God asked for someone to speak for Him and Isaiah replies, "Here am I! Send me." God then tells him that His patience with

---

62   Miller, John W., *Meet the Prophets*, Paulist Press, New York, 1987, p 97,98

63   Leclerc, Thomas L., *Introduction to the Prophets*, Paulist Press, New York, 2017, p 172

64   Smith, William, *A Dictionary of the Bible*, Thomas Nelson, Nashville, 1996, p 267

Israel and Judah was at an end. Only a remnant of the people will survive the invasion of a foreign power.

Isaiah follows the criteria for being called as a prophet in that he comes from the people; goes in a vision to see God; God places His word in Isaiah, and then Isaiah is equipped to speak by having his mouth cleansed.

Isaiah's Convictions

Isaiah sees both Judah and Israel as one country, as it was under Kings David and Solomon. In his life he sees, in c. 734 B.C., Syria and Israel attack Judah in the hope that the three could overcome Assyria (Isaiah 7). Judah turns to Assyria for help against the advice of Isaiah and Assyria invades Syria and takes the northern territories of Israel (II Kings 15:29). In c. 721 B.C. Assyria captured and annexed the rest of Israel and deported much of the population, replacing them with desert peoples (II Kings 17, 18). Isaiah saw his country turn to the Lord after King Hezekiah took the throne (II Kings 18:5). In c. 714 B.C. Isaiah saw the downfall of the Philistine city, Ashdod, who had ceased paying tribute to Assyria and in c. 701 B.C. when Judah ceased paying tribute to Assyria and Sennacherib took 46 Judean cities, but was unable to capture Jerusalem (II Kings 19:35, 36).

God showed Isaiah that 200 years in the future, Cyrus and his Medes and Persians would come and invade Babylon and ultimately release the Jews for their return to their homeland under Davidic kingship (Isaiah 40-55).

Isaiah, Chapters 56-66 cover Isaiah's criticism of idolatry in Israel and the ultimate restoration of Israel under the Redeemer Jesus Christ.

"The Redeemer will come to Zion,
And to those who turn from transgression in Jacob,"
Says the Lord.
Isaiah 59:20

Chapter 22

Micah

The Life and Culture of Micah

Micah is known only as having resided in the village of Moresheth. Moresheth-Gath, near Lachish, was one of the protector cities surrounding Jerusalem and was about 23 miles south and west of Jerusalem, located on the slopes near the coastal plain.

Micah lived during the reign of Kings Jotham, Ahaz, and Hezekiah (Micah 1:1). Jeremiah 26:18 tells us that he prophesied during the days of King Hezekiah of Judah.

Miller postulates that Micah may have been an elder in Moresheth, possibly even a chief elder[65].

Micah, a contemporary of Isaiah, saw the Syro-Ephraimite war against Judah, and felt the presence of the Assyrians to the north. At his times of prophecy (approximately 715-687 B.C.) much of the northern country of Israel was already under the control of Assyria. Samaria had fallen to Assyria in c. 722 B.C., Ashdod in c. 711 B.C., and Jerusalem was besieged in c. 701. B.C. Miller[66] suggests that the bulk of Micah's prophecies occurred just prior to the events in c. 701 B.C.

Micah's Calling

The only clue to Micah's calling to prophecy is found in Micah 3:8. He is "full of power by the Spirit of the Lord, and of justice and might, to declare to Jacob his transgression and to Israel his sin."

---

65   Miller, John W., *Meet the Prophets*, Paulist Press, New York, 1987, p 125
66   Miller, John W., *Meet the Prophets*, Paulist Press, New York, 1987, p 127

Micah was separating himself from the prophets who prophesied for money (Micah 3:8)

Micah meets the criteria for a prophet because he speaks the word of the Lord, and his prophecies are fulfilled.

Micah's Convictions

Micah prophesied of Samaria and Jerusalem (Micah 1:1), the capital cities of Israel and Judah. He foretold the upcoming judgment of Israel, and that Samaria was to become a "heap of ruins" (Micah 1:6).

Jerusalem was to be attacked to the very gates in Micah 1:9, even as other "prophets" were prophesying that Jerusalem was sacrosanct and untouchable.

He speaks against the worshiping of idols and the coming judgment in Micah 1:3-7.

Like Amos, Hosea, and Isaiah, Micah decries the injustice of the rich and their oppression of the poor. In Micah 2:2, he tells of the rich forcibly seizing land, taking the inheritance and ability to survive from the common people. He rails against corrupt leaders and judges taking bribes for a judgment; priests charging to teach; and prophets charging for "divining" and prophesying peace in Micah 3:5-7 and 3:11.

Because of these corrupt leaders, Micah sees that Jerusalem will "become a heap of ruins" (Micah 3:12).

Micah then tells of Jerusalem's future in the latter days. Jerusalem will again be the House of God; peace will reign, and a remnant of the people will be made a strong nation (Micah 4:1-7). Chapter 5 tells of the coming Messiah (Micah 5:2-5) and of God's deliverance from the Assyrians (Micah 5:5-13).

In chapters 6 and 7 Micah presents God's case against the people and confesses their sins.

He has shown you, O man, what is good;
And what does the Lord require of you
But to do justly,
To love mercy
And to walk humbly with your God?
Micah 6:8

Chapter 23

Zephaniah

The Life and Culture of Zephaniah

Zephaniah was the son of Cushi, the son of Gedeliah, the son of Amariah, the son of Hezekiah (Zephaniah 1:1). While Amariah is not listed as a son of King Hezekiah, most Biblical scholars assume that the Hezekiah mentioned is King Hezekiah, making Zephaniah of royal blood[67]. Zephaniah's father, Cushi, was possibly an Ethiopian, since the word Cushi means "an Ethiopian".

Zephaniah was probably raised during the reign of the evil King Manasseh and then prophesied during the beginning years of King Josiah, before the reformation began.

Zephaniah prophesied under King Josiah who reigned from approximately 640-609 B.C.

We do not know where he lived in Judah, or what his former occupation might have been.

Assyria had moved her capital from Ashur to Nineveh, and Judah was one of her vassal states, as were Egypt and Babylon. In c. 668 B.C., Assurbanipal had succeeded Esarhaddon in Assyria and was challenged by Babylonia to the east, Egypt and Greece from the south and west, and northern nomadic tribes.

King Manasseh of Judah was unlike his father, King Hezekiah. While Hezekiah had followed the Lord, King Manasseh erected idols and altars in all the high places and even in the temple of God (II Kings 21:3-7).

---

[67]   Hailey, Homer, *A Commentary on the Minor Prophets*, Baker Book House, Grand Rapids Michigan, 1972, p 222

Zephaniah's Calling

There is no record in the scripture that tells of Zephaniah's calling to be a prophet, only that "The word of the Lord came to Zephaniah".

Zephaniah meets the criteria for prophecy because he speaks the word of the Lord, and his prophecies are fulfilled

Zephaniah's Convictions

Zephaniah begins his prophecies by foretelling judgment on the world and Judah in verses 1:2-6 because of idol worship. He proclaimed against those who worship Baal in Jerusalem; those "Chemarim" (priests of Baal); the Jewish priests who had been unfaithful; the star worshippers; those who swear by both Jehovah and Milcom; and those who "turn back" from the Lord.

In verses 1:7-2:3 Zephaniah explains what catastrophes will occur in the day of the Lord. On that day God will judge the world and purge it with fire. He urges Judah to repent.

Zephaniah 2:4-2:15 tells of the destruction of Philistia, Moab and Ammon, Ethiopia and Egypt, and Assyria. Chapter 3 warns Judah that they can only be saved if they turn once again to God. He then prophesies that the return of the remnant will result in the people being cleansed, and the "King of Israel" would be in their midst, referring to the Messiah.

The great day of the Lord is near;
It is near and hastens quickly.
The noise of the day of the Lord is bitter;
There the mighty men shall cry out.
Zephaniah 1:14

Chapter 24

Nahum

The Life and Culture of Nahum

Nahum came from a town called Elkosh, possibly located just north of the Dead Sea. His ministry occurred from approximately c. 630-612 B.C.[68] Nahum does not mention his occupation, his family, or the kings under whom he served.

In c. 721 B.C. Samaria was taken by Sargon II of Assyria and the people were deported to slavery in Assyria. In c. 701 B.C. much of Judah was captured by Sennacherib and the Assyrian army and placed under vassalage. In c. 663 B.C. Thebes, in Egypt, was captured by the Assyrians under Assurbanipal. The city was ravaged, babies were smashed into the ground, men were placed on stakes and others were flayed and their skins covered the city walls, with their heads stacked into pyramids. All the treasures of the city were taken to Nineveh.

In Nahum's time, much of the known world was under the dominion of Assyria. They dominated by force and the threat of cruelty.

Nahum's Call

Nahum 1:1 tells us that this book was written as a result of a vision by Nahum. His criteria for being called as a prophet is confirmed in that he proclaimed his vision and his prophecies came true.

---

[68]   Hailey, Homer, *A Commentary on the Minor Prophets*, Baker Book House, Grand Rapids Michigan, 1972, p 2250

Nahum's Convictions

Nahum wrote of God's wrath and anger toward Assyria. He predicted the fall of Nineveh, the capital city of Assyria, and the release of Judah's vassalage in Nahum 1:2-13. In chapters 2 and 3 Nahum describes the destruction of the city by the Babylonians. Assyria would be destroyed just as Thebes had been."

Nahum is careful to attribute the machinations of their defeat to God, even though Babylon provided the soldiers in Nahum 2:13 and 3:5.

"God is jealous, and the Lord avenges;
The Lord avenges and is furious.
The Lord will take vengeance on His adversaries,
And He reserves wrath for His enemies."
Nahum 1:2

Chapter 25

Habakkuk

<u>The Life and Culture of Habakkuk</u>

In c. 612 B.C. Babylonians, Medes, Chaldeans, Persians, and Cimmerians attacked Nineveh and defeated the Assyrians.

King Josiah died in approximately 609 B.C. after a battle against Pharaoh Necho and Egypt. His son Jehoahaz reigned for only three months (II Kings 23:32) and was deposed at the command of Pharaoh Necho by Eliakim, called Jehoiakim, Jehoahaz's brother. Both sons of Josiah worshiped idols and did evil in the sight of the Lord.

Pharaoh Necho went to war against the Babylonians at Carchemish in 605 B.C. and was defeated, bringing Judah under the rule and vassalage of Babylon.

Habakkuk does not mention either his family or former occupation. Hailey[69] suggests that the book must have been written about 606 B.C. LeClerc[70] suggests a ministry of c. 605-598 B.C. Both scholars speculate that Habakkuk may have been a temple prophet with a Levitical background based on his writings in chapter 3.

<u>Habakkuk's Call</u>

There is no story of his call to prophesy. Verse 1:1 explains that he was a prophet when he witnessed his burden, or oracle—his divine announcement.

Habakkuk fills the criteria of being a biblical prophet because he speaks the word of God and his prophecies come to pass.

---

[69]   Hailey, Homer, *A Commentary on the Minor Prophets*, Baker Book House, Grand Rapids Michigan, 1972, p 272

[70]   Leclerc, Thomas L., *Introduction to the Prophets*, Paulist Press, New York, 2017, p 234

Habakkuk's Convictions

Habakkuk speaks with God. In verses 1:2-4 he asks God why He seems to allow the unrighteous to perform violence and injustice.

In verses 1:5-11, God answers. He tells Habakkuk that He is not allowing the unrighteous to get away with their sins, but is sending the Babylonians (Chaldeans) to take care of the problem.

In verses 1:12-17, Habakkuk tells God that even though He is holy, why does He allow treacherous men to "swallow up" Judah?

God replies in verses 2:1-5 that God is giving the Judeans time to run after they read Habakkuk's vision. After that, destruction will come, and soon. The righteous God will not judge the people indiscriminately but will save the righteous.

Chapter 2 concludes with 5 woes for the Chaldeans:

1) Woe to those who build their empire by taking from others.

2) Woe to those who build their empire by violence and cruelty.

3) Woe to those who use slavery to build their empire.

4) Woe to those who use intoxicants to mistreat and degrade others.

5) Woe to those who worship idols made of wood or stone and not the true God.

Chapter 3 covers a "psalm" that reminds us and God of His mercy and greatness: His mercy on His people and His greatness in conquering His enemies. He concludes with a song of praise, explaining that he has confidence that God would strengthen him and protect him, even if food fails to produce.

Yet I will rejoice in the Lord,
I will joy in the God of my salvation.
Habakkuk 3:18

Chapter 26

Obadiah

<u>Background</u>

Jacob and Esau were twins with extreme enmity. They were completely different from birth. Jacob stole Esau's birthright (Genesis 27), and was forced to flee for his life. Eventually, (Genesis 33) they meet on positive terms, and Jacob resides in Canaan, and Esau in Seir, which becomes Edom, south of Canaan in the mountainous desert.

Four hundred plus years later, Edom refuses Israel the right to pass through Edom on their way into Canaan, the Promised Land (Numbers 20:14-21). King Saul battled Edom (I Samuel 14:47) and King David made them his subjects (II Samuel 8: 13-14). King Hadad, of Edom became the adversary of King Solomon (I Kings 11:14).

King Amaziah of Judah killed 10,000 men of Edom, captured another 10,000 men of Edom and threw them off a cliff (II Chronicles 25:11-12).

When the Babylonians sacked Jerusalem, the Edomites assisted in the looting of Jerusalem (II Chronicles 21:8-18).

Fuhr and Yates[71] state that the lack of natural boundaries between Edom and Israel contributed to this conflict, as well.

<u>The Life and Culture of Obadiah</u>

Obadiah does not write of his family or occupation, or of which king or kings he served under. It is generally thought that he wrote his book during the lifetime of Jeremiah, around 586-553 B.C., but

---

[71] Fuhr, Richard Alan and Yates, and Yates, Gary E., The Message of the Twelve: Hearing the Voice of the Minor Prophets, B&H Academic, Nashville, 2016 p.148

other scholars point out that Obadiah's writing language pertains closer to c. 846 B.C.

Obadiah's Call

Obadiah 1 tells us that this book was written as a result of a vision by Obadiah. His criteria for being called as a prophet are confirmed in that he proclaimed his vision and his prophecies came true.

Obadiah's Convictions

Obadiah wrote of the future destruction of Edom, due to her mistreatment of her "brother" Israel. No matter where they hid in the mountains, God would deliver them into destruction (Obadiah 2-10).

Obadiah begins his "You should not haves" with verse 11: You should not have rejoiced in Jerusalem's suffering (verse 12); You should not have entered the city and pillaged it (verse 13); You should not have captured the fleeing survivors and turned them over to the Babylonians (verse 14).

Verse 15 begins with a promise of retribution on the day of the Lord. Verses 16-21 tell of the return of Israel and their eventual occupation of Edom, all the way to the Negev.

The day of the Lord is near for all nations.
As you have done, it will be done to you;
Your deeds will return upon your own head.
Obadiah 15

Chapter 27

Jeremiah

Background

Manasseh was king of Judah from c. 698-642 B.C. He allowed idols to be built, even in the temple sanctuary. He ruled for fifty-five years (II Kings 21:1). His son, Amon, became king and ruled for two years, following in his father's footsteps by worshiping idols and forsaking God, before being assassinated by his officials. The officials crowned eight-year-old Josiah as king in c. 627 B.C. Josiah "walked in the ways of David". In 609 B.C., a scroll was found in the temple and read to Josiah. He had his people consult with a prophetess, Huldah, who told them that Judah was to become a disaster after Josiah was dead (II Kings 22).

The country of Israel had been under Assyrian control for over 100 years. Assyria and Egypt were allies, and when Egypt came north to assist Assyria in their war against Babylon, Judah attempted to stop the Egyptians (II Kings 23:29). King Josiah was killed in the battle, and his son, Jehoahaz, became king for only three months before being replaced by his brother, Eliakim, by Pharaoh Neco. The Pharaoh changed Eliakim's name to Jehoiakim (II Kings 23:34).

In c. 605 B.C., Egypt and Assyria were defeated by Babylonia and Crown Prince Nebuchadnezzar at Carchemish. Judah came under the control of Babylon and rebelled against Babylon in c. 597 B.C., and Nebuchadnezzar swiftly attacked Judah and put Jerusalem under siege. During the siege, Jehoiakim died (possibly assassinated), and his son Jehoiachin became king and shortly after surrendered to Nebuchadnezzar (II Chronicles 36:9).

<u>Jeremiah's Life and Culture</u>

Jeremiah was born around c. 648 B.C. in the town of Anathoth, which is about three miles north of Jerusalem, located in the territory allocated to the tribe of Benjamin in the former land of Israel. His father was Hilkiah, the high priest in Judah during the reign of King Josiah. Hilkiah was the High Priest who discovered the Book of the Law in the temple as it was being renovated and re-consecrated after the evil reigns of Kings Manasseh and Amon, who had desecrated the temple of God by placing altars and idols in it. (2 Kings 22, 2 Chronicles 34).

Anathoth was a city given to the Levites in Joshua 21:18. In I Kings 2:26-27, Abiathar was demoted by Solomon from being one of the two High Priests and sent to Anathoth. Abiathar could trace his ancestry back to Eli, and then back to the tribe of Levi in Exodus 32:29. This was a city rich in Levitical tradition and where priests lived who had previously served and officiated at the temple in Jerusalem[72] prior to the reign of Manasseh.

Jeremiah would have been brought up in the priestly tradition, with the education required for a priest. He would have been able to read and write, both in Hebrew and Aramaic, and have understood history and science.

<u>Jeremiah's Call</u>

Jeremiah 1:4-19 tells of his call by God to be a prophet. Jeremiah was a young man in c. 627 B.C., in the 13th year of King Josiah. He was approximately 20 years old when the Lord spoke to him and told him that he had been called before he was born. Jeremiah replies that he does not know how to speak because he is only a child (Jeremiah 1:6).

---

[72]   Miller, John W., *Meet The Prophets*, Paulist Press, New York, 1987 p 158

God touches Jeremiah's mouth and tells him that He has put the words in his mouth. He is sent to "be appointed over nations and kingdoms to uproot and tear down, to destroy and overthrow, to build and to plant" (Jeremiah 1:10). God gives Jeremiah two visions: the branch of an almond tree, representing for Jeremiah to be watchful, and that of a boiling pot, tilting away from the north, representing disaster from the north. God then gives Jeremiah protection by promises of rescue. Jeremiah follows the criteria of a prophet because he is called from the people; God came to him; God's word was placed in his mouth; he speaks back to God; and he is equipped for his assignments.

Jeremiah's Convictions

Jeremiah was a prophet from the approximate age of 20, from c. 627 B.C.to age approximately 60[73], until the destruction of Jerusalem in 586 B.C. by Babylon and Nebuchadnezzar, and then on into c. 569 B.C.

Jeremiah suffered for his convictions. He was threatened with death by the men of Anathoth (Jeremiah 11:21); he was beaten and placed in stocks by the priest Pashur for prophesying (Jeremiah 20:1-2); priests demanded his death for foretelling the destruction of Jerusalem (Jeremiah 26:7-11); he was restricted from going to the temple (Jeremiah 36:5); he and his scribe, Baruch, were forced into hiding (Jeremiah 36:19); all his writings were destroyed by King Jehoiakim (Jeremiah 36:23); he was arrested, beaten, and imprisoned (Jeremiah 37:12-16); he was put under "courtyard arrest" (Jeremiah 37: 21); he was thrown into a cistern full of mud and left to die (Jeremiah 38:6); and he was forced to leave Judah and go to Egypt (Jeremiah 44:28).

Jeremiah prophesied against the idolatry of the Judeans and the injustice of the poor (Jeremiah 2, 3). He prophesied of the destruction

---

[73]   www.generationword.com/notes/Jeremiah/prelim-notes.pdf p1

of Jerusalem by Babylon as early as Jeremiah 4:5, and even how it was to occur in chapter 33. He predicted that those carried to Babylon would be there for 70 years (Jeremiah 29:10). In chapters 30 and 31, he predicted the return of the people and the restoration of Israel and Judah.

During his life, he wrote, through Baruch, the books of Jeremiah, Lamentations, possibly I and II Kings, and possibly Psalm 119.

It is uncertain how Jeremiah died. There are three scenarios listed as to how Jeremiah died: 1) he was stoned by the Jews in Egypt; 2) he died in Egypt; 3) he is removed from Egypt to Babylon after Egypt is conquered by Nebuchadnezzar[74].

"For I know the plans I have for you', declares the Lord,
"Plans to prosper you and not harm you,
Plans to give you a hope and a future."
Jeremiah 29:11

---

[74] www.generationword.com/notes/Jeremiah/prelim-notes.pdf p8

Chapter 28

Ezekiel

Background

In c. 609 B.C., Jehoiakim assumed the throne of Judah. He reigned for eleven years. Jeremiah 26:20-24 explains that King Jehoiakim was responsible for the murder of the prophet Uriah. The king was known for his dishonesty, oppression, and extortion (Jeremiah 22:13-17). Babylon was now the world power, having fought Egypt at Carchemish in c. 605 B.C. and assumed the control of Judah from the conquered Egyptians. Among those taken then were Daniel, Hananiah (Shadrach), Mishael (Meshach), and Azariah (Abednego). In c. 601 B.C. King Jehoiakim rebelled against Babylon and King Nebuchadnezzar of Babylon put Jerusalem under siege. In c. 597 B.C. Jehoiakim died or was assassinated, and King Jehoiachin ascended the throne. Three months later he surrendered to King Nebuchadnezzar.

The army of Babylon stripped Jerusalem of all the treasures of the temple and of the king, and carried into exile 10,000 Judean soldiers, craftsmen, artisans, and officials of the kingdom, including King Jehoiachin (II kings 24:14-17). Only the poor were left in Jerusalem and the surrounding countryside. Among those taken then was Ezekiel.

King Nebuchadnezzar set King Jehoiachin's uncle, Mattaniah, as king of Judah and changed his name to Zedekiah. In King Zedekiah's ninth year, c. 588 B.C., he rebelled against King Nebuchadnezzar. Jerusalem was put under siege, and two years later, in c. 586 B.C., Jerusalem fell. King Zedekiah was captured and forced to watch his sons being killed, and then he was blinded and exiled to Babylon.

Jerusalem's walls were broken down; the temple and the king's palaces were set afire. The chief priest and his assistants and others were taken captive and executed (II Kings 18-21).

Gedaliah was then appointed as "caretaker" of the remaining Judaites by King Nebuchadnezzar. Gedaliah advocated peace with Babylon and was assassinated by Ishmael bar Nethaniah, who was of royal blood (II Kings 25:25).

Ezekiel's Life and Culture

Ezekiel was the son of Buzi, a priest, and therefore would have been in his apprenticeship for the priesthood when he was exiled to Babylon. While most scholars of the time preached that the exile would only last two years before they were returned to Jerusalem, Jeremiah had foretold of the destruction of Jerusalem and the temple just prior to the deportation of the elite. Ezekiel may have been present when Jeremiah spoke.

He was exiled to Babylon when he was 25 years old, five years before he was to have become a temple priest in Jerusalem. His group was sent to live in Nippur, just south of Babylon, near the Chibar River. He may have been placed in Tel Abib, a city that had been flooded, destroyed, and abandoned years before. This would have been a stark contrast to his relatively luxurious home in Jerusalem.

Ezekiel's Call

When Ezekiel was 30 years old, the year he would have become a priest (Numbers 4:3), he saw a vision of God five years into his exile. Ezekiel 1-3 tells of his visions of the glory of God in the heavens. The glory of God was surrounded by four cherubim, angels with four wings and four faces, and with wheels within wheels (Ezekiel 1:4-24). God spoke to him, and he fell facedown (Ezekiel 1:25-28).

Ezekiel received his call in chapters 2 and 3. God calls him "son of man", meaning "mortal". He tells Ezekiel that he is being sent to the Israelite exiles in Babylon, a "rebellious people". He was to relate what God tells him to say, whether they will listen or not.

In his vision, God placed an open scroll in front of him. The scroll was filled with lamentations, mourning, and woes. He was told to eat the scroll. It tasted of sweetness, like honey.

He is told again to go to the exiles and speak God's words to them. God equips Ezekiel with a hard head and the courage to go to the people.

Ezekiel heard God's heavenly chariot leave, and then went to his people and became stuporous and overwhelmed for seven days.

Ezekiel's Convictions

The Book of Ezekiel can be divided into three separate sections: before the siege of Jerusalem in c. 593-589 B.C. (chapters 1-23), during the siege of Jerusalem (c. 585-586 B.C.) and after the fall of Jerusalem in c. 586 B.C. until c. 572 B.C.

Before the Siege

Ezekiel chapter 4 seems to have occurred about fourteen months after his calling visions. God tells him to enact the siege of Jerusalem using a clay brick as Jerusalem and small siege equipment. He was also to use an iron pan to illustrate the strength of the siege. After completing this task, he was to lie on his left side for 390 days and then on his right side for 40 days. It is thought[75] that the 390 days represented the period from Solomon's unfaithfulness to Jerusalem's fall, and the 40 days represent the wicked reign of Manasseh. During this time, he was to eat only a vegetable diet, as if he, also, was being besieged. He was to shave the hair off his head and beard, and focus on the sins of Jerusalem and Judah, and realize that Jerusalem was going to be destroyed.

---

75   *The NIV Study Bible*, Zondervan Corporation, 1985 p 1234

His next vision occurred while he was seated at his home in Tel Abib with the exiled elders of Judah (Ezekiel 8). God led him to see the temple in Jerusalem. The people had again brought idols into the temple and were worshiping them there. God explained that everyone who had not worshiped idols would be spared, but everyone else would be killed (Ezekiel 9). Chapter 10 tells of the glory of God leaving the temple and ascending to heaven. Chapters 11-24 tell of the leaders of Jerusalem telling the people of Jerusalem it is time to build when, in fact, it was time to run. In the vision, Ezekiel sees the King being captured by the Babylonians, blinded, and exiled to Babylon. God tells Ezekiel that most of the Jerusalemites will be killed, and that the remaining House of Israel is to be the captives in Babylon and other parts of Babylonia. They will return, remove the idols and again worship God in the temple. God further points out that Babylon is God's sword, and will be removing the idolatrous people from the land. In Ezekiel 24:15, God tells Ezekiel that his beloved wife is going to die and that he cannot mourn her because on the same day the temple of God in Jerusalem was burned. It was a sign that God was in control and that He was the Lord (Ezekiel 24:27).

During the Siege

Chapters 25-32 relate Ezekiel's oracles or visions of the future humiliation and conquest of the countries of Ammon, Moab, Philistia, Tyre, and Egypt. They, too, will fall under Babylon's military.

After the Siege

While chapters 1-32 were primarily a message of destruction and death, chapters 33-48 became a message of hope for those who will follow God. These chapters follow the message that Jerusalem had fallen (Ezekiel 33:21-22).

God assigns Ezekiel as watchman for the Jewish exiles in Babylonia. He is to warn them of the consequences of their sin and idolatry and prepare them for the return to Israel. Chapter 24 requires the "shepherds" or leaders of the people to begin leading. In chapter 37, God tells Ezekiel that Israel and Judah will again become one nation under one king. Chapters 38-39 explain that world powers will again attack Israel, but Israel will be protected by God. Chapters 40-47 give the plans for the rebuilding of the temple in Jerusalem. From 47:13-48:35 deals with the allocations of the tribes of Israel.

Ezekiel prophesied for twenty-two years, until c. 571 B.C. According to Muslim tradition, he is buried in modern day Iraq near the village of Kefil[76].

"As surely as I live, declares the Sovereign Lord,
I will rule over you with a mighty hand and an outstretched arm
And with outpoured wrath.
I will bring you from the nations
And gather you from the countries where
you have been scattered
With a mighty hand and an outstretched arm
And with outpoured wrath."
Ezekiel 20:33

---

[76]   https://en.wikipedia.org/wiki/Ezekiel

Chapter 29

Haggai

Background

Nebuchadnezzar had stripped Judah of many of the Jews. Daniel was taken into captivity in c. 605 B.C., and Ezekiel in c. 597 B.C. God used these men to give hope and direction to the Jewish exiles.

Nebuchadnezzar died in c. 562 B.C., In c. 549 B.C., Nabonidus, King of Chaldea (Babylonia), left his god, Marduk, and Babylon and began worshiping the moon god, Sin, in northern Arabia. He left his son, Belshazzar, in charge of Babylon and the surrounding area. In c. 539 B.C., Cyrus, a Persian, had defeated the Median king, combined their militaries, and attacked and conquered Babylon. He appointed as governor Darius the Mede, whose real name was probably Gubaru (Darius means "lord")[77].

In c. 538 B.C., Cyrus issued a decree to allow Jews to return to their land (II Chronicles 36 and Ezra 1). Sheshbazzar, a "prince of Judah", brought back the stolen articles from the temple, gold and silver from the Jews not returning at this time, and approximately 50,000 Jewish exiles from Babylon to Jerusalem (Ezra 1-2). Zerubbabel, the grandson of King Jehoiachin, was sent as governor of the land in c. 520 B.C. He brought with him Joshua, the High Priest.

Both these groups received resistance to their return from those Jews who had not been exiled, by Samaritans, and by "people of the land" who now occupied homes and farms around Jerusalem and all of Judah. Because the non-exiles were considered unclean by the returning exiles, even more disparity occurred between the groups. Also, there were issues because some of the returning exiles had

---

[77]   Hailey, Homer, *A Commentary on the Minor Prophets*, Baker Book House, Grand Rapids Michigan, 1972, p 299

brought their non-Jewish spouses and children with them. These were also considered unclean.

Those exiles considered clean were able to build the altar and foundation for the temple before resistance halted the effort. Things were not as the exiles had thought: and the city walls were nothing but rubble, the houses were burned. Much of the land had not been cultivated for over 50 years.

In Babylon, Cambyses ruled from c. 529-522 and during his reign he attempted to capture Egypt, but was forced to return to Babylon to put down rebellions and revolts. Darius I, Hystapes, took over in c. 522 B.C. and ruled until c. 486 B.C.

The Life and Culture of Haggai

It is assumed that Haggai returned to Judah from exile in Babylon. Because he spoke mainly to Governor Zerubbabel and High Priest Joshua, it is thought that he may have been a court prophet. Based on Haggai 2:3, Haggai may have seen the original temple prior to it being looted and burned. If this is true, then Haggai probably would have been in his 70's.

Haggai's Calling

Ezra 5:1-2 and Ezra 6:14-16 tell us that Haggai was a prophet. Haggai 1:1 tells us that the "word of the Lord came through the prophet Haggai", c. August 29th, 520 B.C[78].

We know nothing else of his calling except that he was called from the people, he listened to the Lord, and spoke it to the people.

---

[78]   *The NIV Study Bible*, Zondervan Corporation, 1985 p 1402

Haggai's Convictions

In Haggai 1:2-11, Haggai asserts that the temple is not completed; not because of the drought, with its poor harvests and lack of food, drink, and heat, but the drought with its lack of food, drink, and heat is because the temple is not completed. He urges Zerubbabel and Joshua to complete the temple. He carried the message to the people and their spirit was stirred. Construction began c. September 21,c.520 B.C.

In chapter 2:1-9, Haggai tells the people that even though the temple may not be as ostentatious as the original Solomonic temple, the Lord is with them in the rebuilding and will bless the new temple.

In Haggai 2:10-19, Haggai explains to the people that they were defiled or unclean because the temple had not been rebuilt, but that now the people needed to repent and be restored to the Lord. The people were to look back at the previous years and see the difference in their lives, now that God was beginning to bless them.

Haggai 2:20-23 tells us that Haggai was promised by the Lord that not only would the temple be blessed, but that the covenant of David would continue through Zerubbabel, the several-times great-grandson of David, to the Messiah (Matthew 1:12,16).

Haggai only prophesied in his book from c. September to December 520 B.C. In those four months, Haggai was able to encourage the people to rebuild the temple and give them hope for a future with God.

I will shake all nations,
And the desired of all nations will come,
And I will fill this house with glory,
Says the Lord God almighty.
Haggai 2:7

Chapter 30

Zechariah

Background

See the background of Haggai for this information.

The Life and Culture of Zechariah

Zechariah was born in Babylon during the exile. He was the son of Berechiah and the grandson of Iddo. Iddo was the head of a family of priests that returned to Jerusalem under the governor Zerubbabel and the High Priest, Joshua, in c. 520 B.C. (Nehemiah 12:4). Nehemiah 12:16 explains that Zechariah was the head of the family, so it seems apparent that his father, Berechiah, possibly died at a young age.

Again, Zechariah returned to the land of his grandfather's birth. He was a priest, but there was no temple in which to worship. The city walls had crumbled, as were family homes. The city of Jerusalem was occupied by Jews who had not been exiled, Samaritans, Ammonites, Arabians, Philistines, and desert peoples, most of whom were unwilling to give up their homes or their way of life, which included worship of false gods, and for the Jews, marriages to other peoples. Much of the land had not been cultivated for two generations, and Israel was experiencing a severe drought (Haggai 1:10).

When the exiles had first returned, an altar had been built where the temple was to be built, and the foundation for the temple structure had been laid. Resistance from the non-Jewish inhabitants, and the lack of dedication from many of the returned exiles, caused a stoppage of the temple construction for about sixteen years.

In the fall of c. 520 B.C., Haggai began to encourage and chastise the people, and they again began working on the temple construction.

Zechariah's Calling

Zechariah, a priest of God, was called by God to be a prophet. God told him that He was angry with the people for rejecting Him, and that He would return to the people if the people would return to Him (Zechariah 1:1-6).

The criteria for being a prophet are met. Zechariah hears the word of the Lord and relays that when and to whom he is told by God.

Zechariah's Convictions

Zechariah begins his prophecies with eight visions from Zechariah 1:7 to 6:8. In each vision, he sees angels who are interpreting the visions. The first vision entails a man on a red horse amidst the myrtle trees. The man declares that God told him that He (God) would return to Jerusalem, and Israel would again become prosperous.

Vision two is of the destruction of the four nations (horns) that have oppressed Israel. (The people of Israel and Judah now consider themselves Israel, not separated as before the exile.) The four nations will be destroyed by four other nations (craftsmen).

Vision three explains that God will be the Protector of the Jerusalem of the future, and because of God's protection, walls would not be needed. Vision four sees the High Priest, Joshua, being removed of filthy clothes and given clean robes and a turban, showing that God is restoring the priesthood as long as the priesthood walks in the way of God. Vision five is an encouragement to Zerubbabel. He started the building of the temple, and he will be able to finish it. Vision six shows a large flying scroll, written on both sides. On one side is a curse against thievery, and the other side curses those who swear falsely.

Vision seven shows a woman in a large basket, representing wickedness. The wickedness is being removed from Israel and sent back to Babylon. Vision eight shows Zechariah four chariots representing the four winds that go forth for God to protect Israel. Following the visions, Zechariah is then told by God to make two crowns. Joshua, the High Priest, is to put one on and then the promise of a King and High Priest to come (the branch) is declared in Zechariah 6:9-15.

Chapters 7 and 8 are encouragements to the people who are building the temple. Zechariah tells the people that they no longer need to fast in response to the destruction of Jerusalem or the temple, because they are being rebuilt, and people from the outside are going to come to Jerusalem to worship at the temple.

Chapters 9-14 focus on the future restoration of Israel, God's protection of the land of Israel, and the Coming Kingdom of the Lord, where He will come and reign over the world.

The Lord will be king over the whole earth.
On that day there will be one Lord
And His name the only name.
Zechariah 14:9

Chapter 31

Malachi

Background

In c. 538 B.C., Cyrus issued a decree to allow Jews to return to their land (II Chronicles 36 and Ezra 1). Sheshbazzar, a "prince of Judah", brought back the stolen articles from the temple, gold and silver from the Jews not returning at this time, and approximately 50,000 Jewish exiles from Babylon to Jerusalem (Ezra 1-2). Zerubbabel, the grandson of King Jehoiachin, was sent as governor of the land in c. 520 B.C. He brought with him Joshua, the High Priest, and others.

Both returning groups received resistance from those Jews who had not been exiled, by Samaritans, and by "people of the land" who now occupied homes and farms around Jerusalem and all of Judah. Because the non-exiles were considered unclean by the returning exiles, even more disparity occurred between the groups. Also, there were issues because some of the returning exiles had brought their non-Jewish spouses and children with them. These, too, were considered unclean.

Those exiles considered clean were able to build the altar and foundation for the temple before resistance halted the effort. Things were not as the exiles had thought: the city walls were in rubble, the houses were burned, and much of the land had not been cultivated for at least two generations.

With the encouragement of the prophets Haggai and Zechariah, the temple was completed in c. 515 B.C.

In c. 458 B.C. Ezra, a priest, returned to Jerusalem from Babylon with a third group of exiles. He attempted to restore and teach a love and respect for the law.

Nehemiah was appointed Governor and managed to complete the city wall repairs around c. 445 B.C.

The Life and Culture of Malachi

With the temple completed, the Jews had expected the prophecies of Jeremiah, Haggai, and Zechariah to already be in effect. By now, Babylon, Egypt, and the Canaanites should have gone away, and God should be blessing Israel. A great grandson of David should be occupying the throne, and immense wealth should be pouring into the Israeli coffers.

Instead, the people were noticing that the evil-doers were prospering (Malachi 3:15); sick and crippled animals were being sacrificed (Malachi 1:8); the priests were mostly corrupt (Malachi 2:8, 9); men were divorcing their wives and marrying foreign women (Malachi 2:11); and people were looking for God (Malachi 2:17, 3:14). The formerly devout Jews had lost hope, and few took the law seriously.

There is no information in the Bible about Malachi's life.

Malachi's Call

Malachi 1:1 calls Malachi's calling an oracle: the word of the Lord through Malachi. This is all we have for a calling. Malachi meets the criteria for a prophet because he speaks as God directs, and the prophecies he makes come true.

Malachi's Convictions

God tells Malachi that if He is to be the Master, then the people must honor Him. They have been sacrificing animals that are corrupt, not even the priests will eat their share (Malachi 1:6-14).

The priests should be an example to the people by honoring God, following the covenant, and teaching the people. Instead, the priests are causing men to stumble and violating the covenant; failing to teach or to be an example for the people (Malachi 2:1-9). Either the priests must begin to do right, or they will be cursed by God (Malachi 2:1-9).

God tells Malachi that He hates divorce. The people are once again divorcing Jewish wives and marrying heathen women. The heathen women always bring their gods with them, breaking God's covenant with them. Anyone who does this will be cut off from God (Malachi 2:10-16).

In Malachi 2:17-3:5 God warns Malachi that judgment is coming to cleanse the priests and to testify against sorcerers, adulterers, perjurers, and those who defraud laborers of their wages, oppress widows and orphans, and take away justice from aliens.

The people have been reluctant to tithe or bring offerings. God has promised to abundantly bless those who have been faithful. Most of the people have given up on worshipping God because they have not been blessed. They have not been blessed because they have given up on God (Malachi 3:7-15).

God told Malachi that He remembers those who have not forsaken Him, those who have not worshiped idols, those who fear the Lord. God will remember them, and people will be able to distinguish them from those who do not fear the Lord (Malachi 3:16-17).

Chapter 4 speaks of the day of the Lord, when judgment of the wicked will take place. The righteous will then have victory over the wickedness of the world. The people of Israel must remember the law of Moses, and before the day of the Lord comes, an Elijah (John the Baptist) will be sent to reconcile families and to point the people back to God.

See, I will send my messenger,
Who will prepare the way before me.
Then suddenly the Lord you are seeking
Will come to his temple;
The messenger of the covenant, whom you desire will come,
Says the Lord Almighty
Malachi 3:1

Chapter 32

Daniel

Background

Daniel (God is my judge), c. 457-362 B.C., was believed to be a descendant of King Hezekiah (Isaiah 39:7)[79]. While not included in the Hebrew Bible under "Prophets", Daniel is known for his prophecies. Most of his prophecies are included in chapters 7-12.

As in Isaiah, some scholars believe that Daniel could not have predicted (prophesied) the correct succession of future world powers, the still-future coming of Christ, and the End of Days. Many of these scholars believe that Daniel wrote chapters 1-6 and 9, and that 7-12 were written by scholars following the Israeli return from Babylon, the ascension of the Greeks, and then Rome.

Daniel's Life and Culture

Daniel was a young man, a prince, when he was captured and taken to Babylon. He was likely born under the aegis of King Josiah, who was responsible for the spiritual awakening of Israel. Lehman Straus calls Daniel a "man of perception, purpose, principle, prayer, purity, and power"[80].

It is likely that Daniel and his companions were made eunuchs, although Daniel does not write about this.

In 626 B.C., Nabopolasser ascended the throne of Babylon, overthrowing the Assyrian empire during his reign. Judah had been

---

[79]   https://www.chabad.org/library/article_cdo/aid/3630049/jewish/Daniel-Prophet-of-the-Bible-His-Life-and-Accomplishments.htm-Berstein, Aurohan

[80]   Strauss, Lehman: The Prophecies of Daniel. (Neptune, New Jersey: Loizeaux Brothers, 1969) p22

under the dominion of Assyria since 670 B.C.; Now they were under Babylonian power.

King Jehoiakim became King of Judah the same year Nabopolasser died, and his son, Nebuchadnezzar became ruler of Babylonian territories, including Judah.

Three years later, King Jehoiakim rebelled against Babylon and went to war with the Chaldeans, Syrians, Moabites, and Ammonites (II Kings 24).

King Jehoiachin, son of Jehoiakim, became king at eighteen years of age after his father's death. Three months later, Jerusalem was besieged and King Jehoiachin, his wives, servants, officers, and princes, along with soldiers, craftsmen, and smiths, were taken to Babylon. Daniel was one of the princes.

Daniel's Calling

Daniel is considered to be a prophet in the Christian faith. He is not considered to be a prophet in the Hebrew Bible or the Jewish faith. A godly man, a man of prayer and faith, Daniel was given a gift of interpreting dreams and visions of the future.

Daniel's Convictions

Daniel begins his captivity by refusing to defile his body with strong drink and rich food.

In chapter 2, he interprets Nebuchadnezzar's dream. He gives the credit to God for his ability to not only know the dream but also to interpret the dream of the four future kingdoms.

Nebuchadnezzar's second dream in chapter 4 was again interpreted by Daniel. This was the dream in which the king takes credit for all of Babylon's victories and accomplishments. A year later, the king is reduced to living and acting like an animal until he recognizes that God is in control.

Chapter 5 tells the story of the writing on the wall. Belshazzar was now king, and while feasting, using the stolen Jewish temple utensils, words began to appear on a wall in the palace.

Daniel was called and interpreted the writing. That night, Belshazzar was slain and Babylon conquered by the Persian army, just as Daniel had prophesied (October 12, 539 B.C.).

In chapter 6, Daniel is thrust into a den of lions because of his worship of God over the worship of Darius, the king.

In chapters 7-12, Daniel has visions of the future. He sees the four future kingdoms, the fate of Israel, and the end times (the tribulation).

Daniel became powerful in Babylon, was visited by the angel Gabriel, and eventually died.

Rabbinic sources place Daniel's death during the reign of Persian King Artaxerxes (Ahasuerus), and Daniel was killed by Haman and most likely buried in Susa, Iran, near Babylon[81].

I have heard of you,
That the Spirit of God is in you,
And that light and understanding
And excellent wisdom are found in you
Daniel 5:14

---

[81]   https://en.wikipedia.org/wiki/Daniel_(biblical_figure)

Chapter 33

John the Baptist

John bar Zechariah

<u>Background</u>

Israel, now under the rule and occupation of Rome, is divided into five small countries: Galilee, Samaria, and Judea on the west bank of the Jordan River, and Decapolis and Perea on the eastern bank.

High Priests, tax collectors, and other high-ranking officials must purchase their way into office. Rome had appointed King Herod (37-4 B.C.) over Judea, Samaria, Galilee, and parts of Perea and Syria. His son, Herod Antipas, ruled from 4 B.C. to 39 A.D. as tetrarch over Galilee and Perea. The Herods were from Idumea, formerly Edom, and were not Israeli.

<u>John's Life, Culture and Calling</u>

John's parents were both of priestly descent from Aaron, Moses' brother. John's mother, Elizabeth, had been barren, and by this time they both were well advanced in years (Luke 1:7). Yet they had continued praying for a child. John's father Zacharias, served as a minister in the temple for one week, twice a year. There were approximately eighteen thousand priests. The incense in the temple was lit twice a day: at 9 A.M. and 3:30 P.M. Each priest was allowed to light the incense only once in his career. It was Zacharias' turn. As he was lighting the incense an angel appeared.

The angel told Zacharias to not be afraid, and announced that his prayer for a child had been heard by God. The angel instructed the priest to name his son John. The angel then explained that John was to be great in the sight of the Lord, filled with the Holy Spirit, and was to turn many Israelites back to the Lord God. The angel added that John was never to drink wine or strong drink, and was to prepare the people for the Lord to come (Luke 1:13-17).

When Zacharias expressed doubt about his and Elizabeth's advanced age, the angel, now known as Gabriel, told Zacharias that he, because of his doubt, would be mute until John was born. As Zacharias left the Holy Place, he was supposed to bless the people, but was unable to speak.

When Elizabeth was six months pregnant, Mary, from Nazareth, visited her aunt Elizabeth. Like Elizabeth, Mary was also with child, but Mary's child would become Jesus of Nazarus. Luke 1:41 tells of John leaping in his mother's womb when Mary entered the home of Zacharias and Elizabeth.

Eight days after John's birth, at his circumcision and naming, the neighbors and relatives expected his name to be Zacharias, as was the custom. Instead, Elizabeth told them his name was to be John. Zacharias confirmed this with a writing tablet. As soon as Zacharias wrote the word John, he was able to speak again. Soon, many people had heard of this miracle, and wondered what manner of child John was to become (Luke 1:57-66).

John's Convictions

John was to become the forerunner of Christ, the Messiah. Some scholars believe that John was an Essene, a semi-ascetic Jewish sect who anticipated the Messiah and practiced baptism[82]. John preached a baptism of repentance for the forgiveness of sin, and that Someone more powerful than he would come to baptize with the Holy Spirit. (Mark 1:4-8).

Jesus traveled from Nazareth to the River Jordan so that He could be baptized by John before entering into the desert to be tempted by Satan.

---

[82]   https://en.wikipedia/wiki/John_the_Baptist

John continued his ministry until he was sent to prison for rebuking Herod Antipas for marrying his brother's wife, Herodias (Luke 3:19, Mark 6:19).

Herodias took offense at John's rebuke and asked that he be killed. Herod feared John, knowing that he was a righteous and holy man (Mark 6:19,20).

During a birthday banquet, Salome, the daughter of Herodias, danced and pleased Herod greatly. When Herod offered her up to half of his kingdom, she asked her mother for directions. Herodias had Salome ask for John's head on a platter. John's head was brought to the banquet.

Tradition explains that the body of John was thrown over the palace wall. His body was taken by his disciples and laid in a tomb (Mark 6:21).

And you, child, will be called
The prophet of the Highest;
For you will go before the
Face of the Lord to prepare His ways,
Luke 1:76

Chapter 34

John of Revelations

<u>Views on John's Identity</u> (??)

Some scholars[83] maintain that John the Apostle could not have written Revelations, explaining that it was most probably written after the death of John the Apostle. Eusebius identified John the Presbyter as the seer of Revelation in his *Church History* (Book III). Some contend that John of Patmos, John the Evangelist, John the Elder, and John the Presbyter could have been separate individuals.

<u>The Culture of John the Apostle</u>

At the time of Jesus and John, Rome had total control over Palestine. Israel was divided into Judea and Samaria, Galilee, Decapolis, Perea, and Iturea with procuratorship of Herod Antipas and Philip. While the Romans ruled the territory, they typically appointed local leaders to rule under them, often selling the position to the highest bidder. These positions included kingship (Herod), the High Priest (Caiaphas), and tax collectors (Matthew), among others.

<u>The Life and Calling of John the Apostle</u>

John was the brother of James and the son of Zebedee and Salome. Salome was most probably the sister of Mary, the mother of Jesus[84]. According to Matthew 4:18-22, Mark 1:16-20, and Luke

---

83   Catholic Encyclopedia: Apocalypse http://www. Newadvent.org/ cathen/015946 Ehrmann, Bart D. (2004) The New Testament: A historical Introduction to the Early Christian Writings, New York: Oxford p.468

84   Topical Bible: Salome (httpa://biblehub.com/topical/s/Salome.htm

5:1-11 tell that Peter, Andrew, and the two sons of Zebedee were fishermen on the Sea of Galilee.

Matthew 4:21 describes John's calling. John and James were fishing with their father when Jesus called them, and they immediately began to follow Him.

Tradition explains that John was the "beloved disciple" and the "disciple whom Jesus loved." If so, then John sat next to Jesus at the Last Supper, followed Jesus to the palace of the High Priest, and stood at the foot of the cross as Jesus was executed. He took Mary, the mother of Jesus, into his care upon Jesus' instruction while on the cross.

John's Convictions

After the Ascension of Jesus and the Holy Spirit's appearance at Pentecost, John and Peter took a leading role in the development of the church. Acts 4:3 records John and Peter being thrown into prison and Acts 8:14 tells of his journey to Minister to the new believers in Samaria, along with Peter. Later, John traveled to Ephesus and helped strengthen the church there. While there, John wrote the letters that ultimately became The First, Second, and Third Epistles of John.

Tertullian writes in *The Prescription of Heretics* that John was banished to Patmos after being plunged into boiling oil and suffering no injury. This occurred during the late first century, under the reign of Emperor Domitian, who was known for his hatred and persecution of Christians.

And you, child, will be called
The Prophet of the Highest;
For you will go before the
Face of the Lord to prepare His ways
Luke 1:76

Chapter 35

Afterword

Prophets were sent by God to guard and protect the people, and to do that by reminding the people of God's mercy and holiness: His mercies are exhibited by the number of times prophets were sent to remind and encourage the people to worship God. God's holiness is displayed as He chastises the people so they will return to Him.

God is protecting and guarding His people by providing someone to speak to them about Him. His holiness is also shown through the prophets. Jeremiah quotes God in Jeremiah 44:4:

> *⁴ However I have sent to you all My servants the prophets, rising early and sending them, saying, "Oh, do not do this abominable thing that I hate!"*
> *⁵ But they did not listen or incline their ear to turn from their wickedness, to burn no incense to other gods. ⁶ So My fury and My anger were poured out and kindled in the cities of Judah and in the streets of Jerusalem; and they [h] are wasted and desolate, as it is this day.'*

And in Jeremiah 29: 17-19:

> *¹⁷ thus says the LORD of hosts: Behold, I will send on them the sword, the famine, and the pestilence, and will make them like rotten figs that cannot be eaten, they are so bad. ¹⁸ And I will pursue them with the sword, with famine, and with pestilence; and I will deliver them to trouble among all the kingdoms of the earth—to be a curse, an astonishment, a hissing, and a reproach among all the nations where I have driven them, ¹⁹ because they have not heeded My words, says the LORD, which I sent to them by My servants the prophets, rising up early and sending them; neither would you heed, says the LORD.*

Besides mercy and righteousness, God is also a God of truth and faithfulness. He warns the prophets of what will happen if they fall away from His worship. Abraham, Moses, and Joshua and all the rest told God's people what would happen if they fell into sin by worshiping idols. God was faithful and true to allow the Israelites to fail and be punished. They were first punished by having other countries subject them to freedom and taxation in the Book of Judges. Later they were deported from their country to Assyria and Babylon for sinning again by idol worship. God was under the same rules as the prophets. He had to tell the truth or He would not be God and they had to tell the truth, or they would not be true to God.

God loves His people, and because He loves them, He gives them opportunities to do right. Both Moses and Joshua warned the Israelites that allowing other peoples to remain in the country would not be beneficial to the well-being of the religious state of the people. Malachi warned the people to marry only among their tribes. Micah prophesied of the upcoming destruction of Judah. The opportunities for the people to do right were there, but because God is loving, the people also had freedom to choose, and because God's holiness requires holiness, He retains the right to discipline His people.

The biblical prophets were messengers of God. Some were farmers, priests, or ranchers; some prophesied in Samaria, Jerusalem, Babylon, or Nineveh; some were old, others young; some died for prophesying what people did not want to hear; some went back to their former occupations; some wrote books, while others left legacies that were ultimately written by others; but all believed in a God of mercy and righteousness.

The Lord is longsuffering and abundant in
mercy, forgiving iniquity and transgression,
but He by no means clears the guilty....
Numbers 14:18

BIBLIOGRAPHY

Fee, G. and Stuart, D., How to Read the Bible for All Its Worth, Grand Rapids, Zondervan, 2003

Fuhr, Richard Alan and Yates, and Yates, Gary E., The Message of the Twelve: Hearing the Voice of the Minor Prophets, B&H Academic, Nashville, 2016

Hailey, Homer, A Commentary on the Minor Prophets, Baker Book House, Grand Rapids Michigan, 1972

Josephus, Flavius, The Complete Works of Josephus, Kregel Publications, Grand Rapids, MI, 19

Leclerc, Thomas L., Introduction to the Prophets, Paulist Press, New York, 2017

McKenzie, John L. Dictionary of the Bible, Simon and Schuster, 1965

Miller, John W., Meet The Prophets, A Beginners Guide to the Books of the Biblical Prophets, Paulist Press, New York, 1987

Muffs, Yochanan, Who Will Stand in the Breach? A Study of Prophetic Intercession, Cambridge, MA: Harvard University Press, 1992

Smith, William, A Dictionary of the Bible, Thomas Nelson, Nashville, 1996

The NIV Study Bible, Zondervan Corporation, 1985

Wolff, Hans Walter, Hosea, Hermeneia , Fortress Philadelphia

Yadin, Yilgal, <u>Hazor II: An Account of the Second Season of Excavations</u>, Magnes Press, Jerusalem, 1956

Internet Sources

https://bibleatlas/abel-meholah/htm

https://christianity.stackexchange.com/questions/15372/what-is-the-religion-of-the-midian-people

https://en.wikipedia/wiki/Astarte

https://en.wikipedia/wiki/Aaron

https://en.wikipedia/wiki/Baal

https://en.wikipedia/wiki/Dagon

https://en.wikipedia.org/wiki/Ezekiel

https://en.wikipedia/wiki/Hadad

https://en.wikipedia/wiki/Marduk

https://en.wikipedia/wiki/Molech

https://en.wikipedia/wiki/Ra

https://en.wikipedia.org/wiki/Shalmaneser_III

http://www.jewfaq.org/origins.htm

Oracc.museum.upenn.edu/amgg/listofdieties/nannasuen

www.biblestudies.com/dictionaries/prophets-prophetesses-prophesy-html

www.bibletools.org/index.cfm/fuseaction/Topical.show/RTD/cgg/ID/2089/Balaam.htm

www.britannica.com/topic/Yahweh

www.britannica.com/biography/Moses-Hebrew-prophet

www.britannica.com/biography/Samuel-Hebrew-prophet

www.chabad.org/library/article_cdo/aid/ https://en.wikipedia.org/wiki/Daniel_(biblical_figure)112050/jewish/The-Prophetess-Deborah.htm

www.chabad.org/library/article_cdo/aid/112396/jewish/Miriam.htm

www.generationword.com/notes/Jeremiah/prelim-notes.pdf

www.Idolphin/Deborah.html.

www.thoughtco.com/chemosh-lord-of-the-moabites

https://www.chabad.org/library/article_cdo/aid/3630049/jewish/Daniel-Prophet-of-the-Bible-His-Life-and-Accomplishments.htm-Berstein, Aurohan

Strauss, Lehman: The Prophecies of Daniel. (Neptune, New Jersey: Loizeaux Brothers, 1969) p22

https://en.wikipedia/wiki/John_the_Baptist

Catholic Encyclopedia: Apocalypse http://www. Newadvent.org/
cathen/015946

Ehrmann, Bart D. (2004) The New Testament: A historical Introduction
to the Early Christian Writings, New York: Oxford p.468

Topical Bible: Salome (httpa://biblehub.com/topical/s/Salome.htm

www.ingramcontent.com/pod-product-compliance
Lightning Source LLC
Chambersburg PA
CBHW051219120626
46547CB00013B/1429